I0181290

READ FASTER
REMEMBER MORE

An Unlimited Learning Book

Conrad Andrews

Cosmic Teapot Publishing

Published by Cosmic Teapot Publishing
Hanmer, ON, Canada
www.cosmicteapot.net
Ordering Information:
Quantity sales. Special discounts are available on quantity purchases by corporations, associations, and others. For details, contact the publisher at the email address above.

To all lifelong learners.

Learning is not the product of teaching. Learning is the product of the activity of learners.

JOHN HOLT

CONTENTS

PART I: PREPARE FOR MORE

FIRST THING

The size of this column will change shortly. It will be a narrow column located in the center of the page. Its purpose is to challenge your reading habits and encourage you to focus on one key aspect of speed reading: controlling eye movement.

Traditionally, we have been taught to word by word; however, this is not the most effective way to read. By altering the text format, we can break away from this habit and focus on controlling the movement of our eyes, or more specifically, minimizing eye movement. This is the first step in unlocking your full reading potential.

As you continue reading this book, you will learn various other important techniques for increasing your reading speed, comprehension, and recall. The path to becoming a proficient reader begins now, and this layout will serve as your starting point. Prepare to revolutionize the way you read!

Before the column changes, though, it's important to know why we're doing this. Generally speaking, there are three things that slow down readers. These are recursion, fixation, and sub-vocalization. Recursion is a term that describes how some readers look back to what they had previously read. Recursion is a hindrance to efficient reading. It can slow down our reading speed and make it harder for us to retain information. This is because it takes longer for the brain to process the data when our eyes move back and forth along a line of text. It also increases the chances of our eyes skipping over important information or getting lost in the text. To improve our reading speed and retention, we need to reduce recursion as much as possible.

In the context of reading, fixation refers to the act of stopping one's eyes on a specific point while reading. It is the process of focusing on a particular word or group of words before moving on to the next. Fixation is an important aspect of reading as it allows the brain to process the information and understand the meaning of the text. However, excessive fixation can slow down reading speed and impede reading efficiency. Speed reading techniques often aim to minimize the number and time of fixations.

The best way to reduce recursion and fixations is by using a technique known as "chunking.[1]" Chunking involves taking in multiple words in one fixation. We pause and gaze briefly in the middle of a few words without moving our eyes. This technique helps you to focus on the meaning of the text rather than the individual terms and allows your eyes to move more smoothly along the text. This is often difficult to do with full lines of text, which is why I'm reducing the column to 1.5 inches. Starting now.

Most books
provide lists
of numbers
or letters to
gradually improve
peripheral vision
and awareness.
However, this
book takes a
unique approach.
Practical
application is the
most effective way
to enhance speed
reading abilities.
That's why this
book integrates
the practice
directly into the
text rather than
solely relying
on traditional
methods. This
allows for a more
natural and

comprehensive learning experience, as you can immediately apply the techniques you learn to actual reading material.

When reading, focus on a spot in the middle of the text and take in the whole line in one glance. Avoid staring for too long and move down each line at a steady pace. Try to minimize the inner-voice that reads to you. With practice, you will be able to increase your reading speed. We will fine-tune these methods throughout the book.

As you progress through the

book, the column of text will gradually widen, challenging you to improve your peripheral vision and awareness. This gradual progression will help you build your skills organically and make it easier to apply the techniques you've learned to your daily reading.

When the width of the text is too much for you to take in with one fixation, it's time to break down the line into two chunks. Depending on the line-length of the text, you should find that one, two, or three fixations are enough.

As you progress through the book, you will learn how to further improve your reading abilities. Not only will you enhance your peripheral vision and awareness, but you will also learn essential techniques for increasing your reading speed. Memory and concentration techniques will also be discussed to help you become an efficient learning machine.

You will also find a unique blend of theory and practice throughout the book. It is a comprehensive guide that will take you on a journey of reading faster, reading smarter, and remembering more. With this guide, you will be able to read more efficiently and effectively and open up new opportunities for your personal and professional life.

GET YOUR MIND READY

Education is not just about memorizing facts and figures; it is about teaching individuals how to learn. In today's fast-paced and ever-changing world, having the ability to learn quickly and effectively is essential. The traditional education system, however, often teaches people what to think rather than how to think. By providing you with the tools to learn, you are empowering yourself to take control of your own education and pave a path to success.

When you learn to learn, you have a skill that will last a lifetime. With this skill, you can grow and evolve. This skill helps you to stay current in your field and adapt to the changing world. You will be able to take on new challenges, explore new areas and make a meaningful impact on the planet. It's about equipping yourself with the skills you need to succeed in life.

Learning how to learn is a process that involves developing

critical thinking skills, problem-solving abilities, and creativity. By fostering these abilities in yourself, you can help yourself become an independent learner who is not afraid to take risks, make mistakes and learn from them. You will be able to process, analyze and evaluate information, and make informed decisions.

Furthermore, teaching yourself how to learn also benefits your mental and emotional well-being. You will develop self-awareness, self-motivation, and self-regulation skills to help you manage your emotions and set goals for your learning journey.

Teaching yourself how to learn is important not only for your academic success but also for your overall well-being and ability to navigate a rapidly changing world. It's time to empower yourself with the ability to learn and give yourself the tools you need to succeed in life.

Despite the importance of learning how to learn, it is unfortunate that many schools and education systems still prioritize teaching students what to think rather than how to think. This means it is up to individuals to take control of their own learning and develop the skills they need to succeed in today's world. However, this can be a rewarding and empowering experience.

Start by setting specific, measurable, and achievable learning goals for yourself. This will give you a clear direction and motivation to keep learning. Once you have your goals, experiment with different learning methods and find what works best for you. Everyone has a unique way of learning, whether it's through reading, watching videos, listening

to podcasts,
or attending
workshops.

Having a curious
mind is one of
the most critical
aspects of learning.
Always be on
the lookout for
new information
and be open to
learning new
things. Instead of
passively receiving
information,
actively engage
with it, ask
questions, make
connections and
apply what you
learn to real-world
situations.

Take time to
reflect on what
you have learned
and how you can
apply it in your
life. Reflecting on
your learning will
help you retain
information better

and improve your understanding. Failure is a natural part of the learning process. Don't be afraid to make mistakes; instead, learn from them and use them as a tool for growth.

By taking control of your own learning, you are setting yourself up for success in today's rapidly changing world. You will be equipped with the skills to adapt, grow and evolve, and you will be able to pave your own path to success. So don't wait for others to teach you how to learn; take control of your own learning today!

We all have the potential to achieve

incredible things, and one of those things is having a powerful memory. Nelson Dellis, a four-time USA Memory Champion, has shown us that anyone can develop a superhuman memory with the right techniques and strategies.

Nelson's journey to becoming a memory champion wasn't an easy one. He faced many challenges but didn't let them stop him from reaching his goal. He began by studying memory techniques, experimenting with different methods, and practicing consistently. With dedication and perseverance, he improved his memory and eventually became a memory champion[2].

His story is a testament to the power of hard work and determination. It shows us that if we set our minds to something, we can achieve it. We may not all want to become memory champions, but we can all benefit from having a better memory. Whether for work, school, or personal development, a powerful memory can give us a significant edge.

Throughout history, there have been countless individuals who have accomplished incredible things through their own determination and hard work. These individuals serve as shining examples of what can be achieved when we set our minds to something and refuse to give up.

Take the story of Malala Yousafzai[3], for example. Despite facing oppression and danger, she became an advocate for girls' education and the youngest Nobel Prize laureate in history. Her unwavering commitment to making education accessible to all serves as an inspiration to us all.

Another example

is that of Helen Keller, who, despite being blind and deaf, became a renowned speaker, author, and advocate for the disabled. Through her perseverance and determination, she was able to overcome her disabilities and make a significant impact on the world[4].

We can also look to figures like Marie Curie, the first woman to win a Nobel Prize and the only person to win the award in two different sciences[5]. Her groundbreaking research in physics and chemistry continues to influence the world today.

These individuals remind us that no matter what obstacles we face, we can all achieve amazing things with hard work and determination. They show us that our limitations are often self-imposed and that with a strong will and a passion for learning, anything is possible.

Every single one of us has the potential to accomplish amazing things. All it takes is a little bit of hard work and determination. But often, we let fear, doubt, and uncertainty hold us back from reaching our full potential.

Think about all

READ FASTER REMEMBER MORE | 21

the things you've
wanted to do but
haven't because
you were afraid
you couldn't do
them. Maybe you've
always wanted
to learn a new
language, start a
business, or take
up a new hobby.
Whatever it is,
don't let fear hold
you back. Believe in
yourself and your
abilities.

It's important
to remember that
success doesn't
come overnight. It
takes time, effort,
and consistency. It
requires sacrifice
and dedication. But
the rewards of hard
work are always
worth it in the end.

Take inspiration
from those who
have accomplished
great things. Look

at successful people and see how they got to where they are. You'll notice that they didn't achieve success overnight. They worked hard, overcame challenges, and never gave up.

When you set your mind to something and work hard towards it, you are capable of achieving anything. You have the power to shape your destiny, create the life you want, and make a difference in the world.

So, don't let fear and doubt hold you back. Believe in yourself and your abilities. Take the first step toward your goal,

and never give up.
With hard work
and determination,
the sky is the limit.
You can accomplish
amazing things.

We all have
the potential to
learn and achieve
incredible things,
but often times
fear and self-doubt
hold us back from
reaching our full
potential. But
what if I told you
that you could
overcome these
fears and learn
anything you want?
This is possible
by following a
few fundamental
principles.

The first step is to
take action. Don't
just sit around and
think about what
you want to learn;
start taking small
steps toward your

goal. And since this book is in your hands, you have taken the first step!

The next step is to be open to experimentation. Don't be afraid to try new things and approach the learning process from different angles. Be open to new methods and techniques and be willing to adapt as you go along.

Learning from failure is an important aspect of this process. Failure is a natural part of the learning process, so embrace and learn from it. Each failure is an opportunity to learn and grow.

Another component is building

confidence. Fear and self-doubt can be debilitating, but your confidence will grow with each small victory and accomplishment. Believe in yourself and your abilities, and don't let fear hold you back.

Finally, it's essential to stay consistent. Learning something new takes time and effort. Keep pushing through, even when it gets tough. Keep practicing and experimenting, and eventually, you'll reach your goal.

By following these principles, you'll be able to overcome your fears and learn anything you

want. Don't let
fear hold you back
from reaching
your full potential.
With hard work,
dedication and
perseverance,
you can achieve
incredible things.

WHAT'S YOUR BASELINE?

Reading is a powerful tool that opens up new worlds, perspectives, and opportunities. The speed at which we read can significantly impact the knowledge and enjoyment we can gain from reading. The faster we read, the more we can read, the more we can learn, and the more we can grow. Improving your reading speed can be a challenging process, but with dedication and practice, you can unlock your full potential as a reader. By increasing your reading speed, you can read more books, articles, and other written materials, which can significantly impact your personal and professional development.

Reading speed is the rate at which a person can read and comprehend written text. The average reading speed for an adult is around 200-300 words per minute (wpm). However, this can vary greatly depending on factors such as education level, occupation, and reading experience.

For example, college-educated individuals tend to have higher reading speeds, averaging around 300-400 wpm. Professionals in fields such as law, medicine, and finance, who are required to read large amounts of technical material, often have even higher reading speeds[6]. On the other hand, people who do not read frequently may have lower reading speeds.

It is also important to note that reading speed can vary depending on the type of material being read. For example, reading a novel or a story can be done at a faster pace, as the focus is on understanding and enjoying the story, while reading a technical manual or a scientific paper requires a slower pace, as the focus is on understanding the information presented.

Many individuals have been recognized for their exceptional reading speed and comprehension abilities. One of the most well-known examples is Kim Peek, who passed away in 2009. Kim was known as the "Mega-Savant of Memory" and could read two pages of a book simultaneously, one page with each eye, at a speed of around 4,000 wpm. He had an extraordinary memory and was able to retain 98% of the information he read, making him a true master of speed reading[7].

Another notable figure in the world of speed reading is Howard Stephen Berg, who holds the Guinness World Record for the fastest reader. He can read up to 25,000 wpm using a technique called Rapid Serial Visual Presentation (RSVP).

RSVP is a technique used to increase reading speed. It involves displaying words or images one at a time, in rapid succession, in the same location on a screen. The technique is based on the idea that the human eye can process a large amount of information when presented in a serial manner rather than in a block format.

The technique works by utilizing

the natural ability of the human eye to follow movement and by eliminating the need for the eye to move back and forth across a page. Instead, the words or images are presented in a stream. The reader's eyes are trained to fixate on one location while the material is presented.

RSVP can be used with a variety of materials, including text, images, and videos. It is commonly used in speed reading programs and can be done online or offline.

It's important to note that RSVP is not recommended for everyone because it may require a certain level of cognitive flexibility and mental effort. The rapid presentation of words may cause strain and fatigue. Moreover, the level of comprehension may be affected by this technique.

While most people will never reach the extremely high reading speeds of Kim Peek or Howard Stephen Berg, it is still possible to tremendously improve one's reading speed. All it takes is dedicated practice.

Determining your baseline reading speed is vital in improving your reading skills[8]. A reading test is an effective way to measure your current reading speed and comprehension level. By taking a reading test, you can establish a benchmark for your reading abilities and set specific goals for improvement.

Various reading tests are available, including timed reading and comprehension tests. Timed reading tests measure how many words you can read in a specific amount of time. In contrast, comprehension tests measure your understanding of the material.

It's important to know that taking a test can be a daunting task. It's normal to feel some level of stress or pressure. Still, it's important to remember that a reading test is just a tool to measure your current abilities and to provide feedback for improvement.

By taking a reading test, you can establish a benchmark for your reading abilities and set specific goals for improvement. With practice, dedication, and the use of speed reading techniques, you can improve your reading speed and comprehension.

To calculate your reading speed from a timed reading test, you will need to measure the number of words in the passage you read and the amount of time it took you to read it. Once you have this information, you can use the following formula to determine your reading speed:

Reading speed (wpm) = Number of words / (Time taken in minutes)

For example, if you read a passage of 250 words in 5 minutes, your reading speed would be:

250 words / 5 minutes = 50 wpm

It's important to note that when doing a timed reading test, you should try to eliminate distractions and focus on the task at hand. Also, it's better to start with a shorter text and gradually increase the length and difficulty as you become more comfortable with the process.

Also, when doing the test, it's good to use a text similar to the materials you will be reading in the future, whether it's fiction, non-fiction, technical or academic text. The texts in this book are general interest articles that will give you some idea about your reading speed and comprehension.

Here is a short piece on the Egyptians for our first reading selection. Following the text, you will find a quick quiz to determine your level of comprehension. Our goal in this book is to improve our reading speed and level of comprehension.

Since this is a baseline test, I have opted to use full-width text. You may even want to revert to the "old fashioned" reading method by moving your eyes along the line and sub-vocalizing. Instead, I would recommend reading it twice. Do it the old way, then try using your new skills. Time both to see how much quicker you already are. Regardless of what you choose to do for this test, you will have a baseline result. This is the number on which we want to improve. We will resume the narrow columns after the quiz.

Just before you start reading, begin timing yourself. Stop your timer as soon as you are done.

Start the timer now!

Egyptian culture is one of the oldest and most fascinating in the world. It dates back to around 5,000 years ago, during the Predynastic period (c. 6000-3150 BCE), and continued to evolve over the course of several millennia.

The origins of Egyptian culture can be traced back to the Nile River Valley, which provided the ancient Egyptians with fertile land for agriculture, as well as a source of water for irrigation. The Nile also played a crucial role in the development of the civilization by facilitating trade and communication between different regions. The regular flooding of the Nile also led to the development of a calendar, which was essential for the organization of agricultural activities.

Around 3100 BCE, the first pharaoh, Narmer, united Upper and Lower Egypt, forming the first centralized state in the history of mankind. This marked the beginning of the Early Dynastic Period, which was characterized by the construction of monumental architecture, the development of hieroglyphic writing, and the rise of theocracy.

Over the centuries, Egyptian culture continued to evolve and develop. The Old Kingdom (c. 2686-2181 BCE) saw the construction of the Great Pyramids and the development of a powerful central government. The Middle Kingdom (c. 2055-1650 BCE) saw a resurgence of art, literature, and religious thought. The New Kingdom (c. 1550-1069 BCE) was marked by the construction of monumental temples and the rise of the pharaohs as god-kings.

The Middle Kingdom of ancient Egypt (c. 2055-1650 BCE) was a period of resurgence and cultural revival after the decline of the Old Kingdom. The capital of Egypt was moved to Thebes, and the pharaohs of the 12th dynasty, who ruled during this time, were able to re-establish central authority and stability. They also focused on the development of art, literature, and religious thought.

One of the most significant achievements of the Middle Kingdom was the construction of large monumental structures, such as the temple complex at Karnack, which was dedicated to the god Amun. This period also saw the rise of the "noble tombs" in the necropolis of Deir el-Bahri, which were decorated with intricate reliefs and inscriptions.

The Middle Kingdom was followed by the Second Intermediate Period (c. 1650-1550 BCE), which was marked by the rise of the Hyksos, a group of foreign rulers who controlled Lower Egypt. They introduced new weapons and technologies, such as the horse-drawn chariot, which had a significant impact on Egyptian military tactics.

The New Kingdom (c. 1550-1069 BCE) was marked by the expulsion of the Hyksos and the reunification of Egypt under the pharaohs of the 18th dynasty. The New Kingdom was a time of great prosperity and territorial expansion, with pharaohs such as Tuthmosis III and Ramses II leading military campaigns in the Near East.

During this period, monumental temples and monumental statues were constructed throughout Egypt, including the temple of Amun at Karnack and the temple of Ramses II at Abu Simbel. The New Kingdom was also marked by the rise of the pharaohs as god-kings, and the development of a powerful central government.

In conclusion, the Middle and Late Kingdom of ancient Egypt were periods of great cultural and political achievements. The Middle Kingdom saw a resurgence of art, literature, and religious thought, and the construction of monumental structures such as the temple of Amun at Karnack. The New Kingdom was a time of great territorial expansion, prosperity and the pharaohs were elevated as god-kings. These periods left a lasting legacy on the civilization and culture of ancient Egypt.

Stop the timer now!

To determine your reading speed, do the following:

Divide 583 by the number of minutes it took you to read the selection.

583 words / ___ minutes = ____ wpm

That is your current reading speed.

Now, let's test your comprehension. Answer ten questions on the content of the article.

1. When did
   the origins of
   Egyptian culture
   begin?
2. What was the
   role of the Nile
   river in the
   development of
   ancient Egyptian
   culture?
3. Who was the first
   pharaoh of Egypt,
   and when did he
   reign?
4. What was the
   significance
   of the regular
   flooding of
   the Nile in the
   development of
   ancient Egyptian
   culture?
5. What was the
   Old Kingdom of
   ancient Egypt
   known for?
6. What was
   significant
   about the Middle

Kingdom of
ancient Egypt?
7. What was one
achievement
of the Middle
Kingdom of
ancient Egypt?
8. Who were the
Hyksos?
9. What was
significant
about the New
Kingdom of
ancient Egypt?
10. What was one
lasting legacy of
ancient Egypt's
Middle and Late
Kingdom?

Answers

1. The origins of Egyptian culture begin around 5,000 years ago, during the Predynastic period (c. 6000-3150 BCE)

2. The Nile River provided the ancient Egyptians with fertile land for agriculture and a source of water for irrigation.

3. The first pharaoh of Egypt was Narmer, who reigned around 3100 BCE.

4. The regular flooding of the Nile led to the development of a calendar that was essential for the organization of agricultural

activities.

5. The Old Kingdom of ancient Egypt is known for constructing the Great Pyramids.

6. The Middle Kingdom of ancient Egypt was a period of resurgence and cultural revival after the decline of the Old Kingdom.

7. The achievements of the Middle Kingdom of ancient Egypt include the construction of large monumental structures, such as the temple complex at Karnack, and the rise of the necropolis of Deir el-Bahri.

8. The Hyksos were a group of foreign rulers who controlled Lower Egypt.
9. The New Kingdom of ancient Egypt was a time of great prosperity and territorial expansion.
10. Lasting legacies include great cultural and political achievements, the resurgence of art, literature, and religious thought, and the construction of monumental structures such as the temple of Amun at Karnack.

Mark your score out of   /10.

How did you do?

Now you can express your reading ability as _____ words per minute with _____ % comprehension. This is your baseline score and what we want to improve on throughout this book. Our goal is to read faster and remember more.

Reading is a powerful tool that can open up a world of knowledge and possibility. However, reading can be a slow and tedious task for many people. But with dedication and the right approach, you can improve your reading speed and comprehension. The key to success is setting goals for yourself.

When it comes to setting goals for improving your reading, it's good to be specific and realistic. Instead of saying, "I want to read faster," set a specific goal, such as "I want to increase my reading speed by 50 words per minute in the next month."

Once you have set your goals, it's important to create a plan of action to achieve them. It's also important to remember that achieving goals is not a one-time event. Remember, it is a continuous process. You will have setbacks and have to adjust your plans. The key is to keep going and keep learning.

A good model for

setting goals is the SMART criteria[9]. SMART is an acronym that stands for Specific, Measurable, Achievable, Relevant, and Time-bound.

Specific: Your goal should be clear and specific. It should answer the questions of who, what, where, when, and why.

Example: I want to increase my reading speed by 50 words per minute in the next month.

Measurable: Your goal should be quantifiable so that you can measure your progress.

Example: I will measure my reading speed by timing myself while reading a passage of text.

Achievable: Your goal should

be realistic and achievable.

Example: I will practice speed reading techniques and set aside dedicated time each day to practice reading.

Relevant: Your goal should be relevant to your overall objectives and align with your values and interests.

Example: Improving my reading speed and comprehension is important to me because I want to read and understand more complex texts in my field of study.

Time-bound: Your goal should have a deadline or a specific time frame in which it should be achieved.

Example: I will achieve my goal

of increasing my reading speed by 50 words per minute within the next month.

Setting goals is not a one-time event; it's a continuous process. You must keep reviewing, adjusting, or developing new goals as you progress.

In summary, the SMART criteria model can help you set clear, specific, measurable, achievable, relevant, and time-bound goals. Using this model can increase your chances of achieving your goals and improve reading speed and comprehension.

MISCONCEPTIONS ABOUT LEARNING

Learning is not confined to the walls of a classroom. It is an ongoing process that can take place anywhere and anytime. It is a journey that can be taken in many different ways, and it is up to each individual to find the path that works best for them. Learning is an essential part of life regardless of age or background. It can be found in simple tasks, such as cooking a meal or tending to a garden. It can be found in the most complex activities, such as mastering a new language or exploring a new culture. It can be found in the books we read, the conversations we have, and the experiences we encounter.

Learning is a way of life, and it is something that should be embraced and celebrated. It is a way to expand our minds, gain knowledge, and grow as individuals. It is a way to explore our passions and discover new interests. It is a way to connect with others and build relationships. Learning is a journey that can take us to places we never thought possible. It is a journey that can open our eyes to the world around us and to the possibilities that exist.

It is a journey that can lead us to a brighter future.

It is true that in our thirties, our brains begin to shrink a little. This process continues into our sixties and often accelerates. The areas most affected are the frontal lobe and hippocampus. As well, cortical density and white matter thin out.

The long-held belief is that this results in cognitive decline. But that isn't true. At least, it doesn't have to be true!

What happens in adulthood isn't set in stone. Cognitive decline isn't a given. Clearly, some people fall victim to aging brains while others maintain their mental sharpness all their lives.

Why?

That's what leads us to our misconceptions[10].

Misconception #1
As we get older, our memories become worse.

The Truth
In healthy individuals, this is only true if we allow it. Let's put it this way: if we never pick up a weight to do a bicep curl, will our biceps be as big as if we worked them out frequently?

Of course not.

If we haven't bothered to learn much since high school, then chances are we haven't had to remember much new information since then, either. Without working out our brains, they won't make new connections. Fortunately, we can start anytime, and our brains will make new connections again.

Initially, it might be difficult to remember new information. Yet, new neural connections can be made very quickly, and our brains will adapt to learning again. With some assistance, it is even possible to be a more effective learner than when we were young.

Misconception #2
Our brains have a fixed number of neural connections and then die off over time.

The Truth
Babies are born with about the same number of connections as an adult. Early in life, there is an explosion

of activity, and then those connections get pruned back around three years old. This explosion happens again in other regions of the brain. Once again, they are pruned.

Those connections can die over time if we don't use them. If we continue to think and learn as adults, we'll likely stay as sharp as we were in our twenties.

The best news, however, is that we can regrow these connections when we start learning again. Learning is the key to neural plasticity. We make new connections constantly, which continues into our old age as long as we use our brains.

The brain is an organ, not a muscle. However, in some

ways, it works like a muscle. If we mentally work out, our brains become more robust and capable. If we do nothing, it weakens, just like a muscle.

Misconception #3

Unlike young learners, adult learners need prior knowledge of something to learn it.

The Truth

In the classroom, one of the first things teachers do when introducing a new topic is activate prior knowledge. Our brains are association machines, so learning something new requires association.

Using prior knowledge helps us to relate and file something new. The information we use as prior knowledge doesn't have to be especially relevant. For example, when I started learning about computer programming, I found it was similar to the building instructions that came with furniture. And while there are some critical differences between the two, this comparison helped frame my learning. Learning is an individual journey that should be tailored to each person's unique style and preferences. Recognizing and embracing this is essential, as it can be the key to unlocking your full potential. Learning should be seen as an opportunity to explore, discover, and grow, not as a chore or a burden.

With the right attitude and approach, learning can be an enjoyable and rewarding experience. Don't be afraid to take risks and try new things, as this can be the best way to learn and grow. Take the time to reflect on what works best for you and use that knowledge to create a learning experience that is tailored to your needs. With the right mindset and dedication, learning can be an incredibly rewarding and fulfilling experience.

MEET YOUR BRAIN

The human brain is an awe-inspiring marvel of complexity and power. It is the epicenter of our nervous system, composed of billions of neurons that work together to control our thoughts, emotions, behavior, and physical movements. It is truly remarkable how this intricate organ can be responsible for so much!

Did you know that the brain is divided into four distinct parts, each with its unique role? The cerebrum is the largest part of the brain. It is responsible for higher-level thinking, such as problem-solving, decision-making, and language. The cerebellum is responsible for coordinating movement and balance. The brainstem controls basic functions such as breathing, heart rate, and digestion. And the hypothalamus is responsible for regulating hormones and controlling our emotions. It's amazing how each part of the brain works together to help us think, move, and feel!

Neurons are the powerhouse of the brain, sending and receiving signals like a complex web of electricity and chemistry. When a neuron receives a signal, it sends an electrical impulse down its axon, triggering the release of neurotransmitters. These neurotransmitters

then travel across
the synapse, the gap
between two neurons,
and bind to receptors
on the next neuron.
This process is repeated
over and over again,
allowing neurons to
communicate with each
other and create the
incredible network that
is the human brain.

The brain is an
incredible organ that
is constantly evolving
and adapting to new
information. This
fantastic process, known
as neuroplasticity, is
responsible for learning,
memory, and even our
thoughts, emotions,
and behavior. With
billions of neurons
communicating, the
brain can form new
connections and
reorganize existing
ones in response to
new experiences. By
understanding how the

brain works, we can gain a better insight into ourselves and the world around us. Neuroplasticity is an incredible phenomenon that allows us to grow and learn, and it's something we should all strive to understand and appreciate.

Neuroplasticity is a fascinating concept that has revolutionized our understanding of the brain and its ability to adapt and change over time. It has been found that the brain can reorganize itself and form new neural pathways throughout life, even in the elderly.

This means that the aging brain is not necessarily doomed to decline but can actually be strengthened and improved with the proper stimulation. One of the most exciting aspects of neuroplasticity is its potential to help the elderly maintain their cognitive abilities. Studies have shown that engaging in activities such as learning a new language, playing a musical instrument, or even just doing puzzles can help to keep the brain active and healthy.

This is because these activities stimulate the brain and encourage the formation of new neural pathways, which can help to preserve cognitive abilities. Another way to keep the brain healthy is to engage in physical activity. Exercise has been found to increase the production of a protein called brain-derived neurotrophic factor (BDNF), which helps to protect neurons and promote the growth of new ones. Exercise also increases blood flow to the brain, which can help to improve cognitive function. Finally, it is vital to maintain a healthy lifestyle. Eating a balanced diet, getting enough sleep, and managing stress can help keep the brain healthy and functioning optimally[11].

Sensory, working, short-term, implicit, and long-term memory are all types of human memory that play a role in how we process information. Each type of memory has its own unique characteristics and functions.

Sensory memory is the first stage of processing information from our senses. It is crucial in how we perceive and interact with the world

around us. It is an
incredibly brief form
of storage, lasting only
a few seconds before
fading away. Still, it
allows us to take in
sensory input from our
environment and store it
temporarily until we can
decide what to do with it.

This type of memory
helps us recognize
patterns or objects
quickly without having
to consciously think
about them, allowing
us to react instinctively
when faced with
familiar situations.
Furthermore, this type
of memory also helps
us remember details
that may be useful later.
For example, suppose
you were walking down
an unfamiliar street
but noticed something
familiar from the corner
of your eye. This could be
sensory memory helping
you recall something you

previously saw[12].

In short, sensory memory is an invaluable tool that helps us process information quickly and efficiently so we can make informed decisions in any given situation.

Working memory is an essential part of the brain's information-processing system. After sensory input is taken in, it is stored in working memory for a short time while we actively think about or manipulate it mentally. This type of memory helps us stay focused on tasks and remember details necessary to complete them successfully - such as instructions or facts needed to solve math problems or finish an assignment.

Working memory plays a vital role in our

ability to concentrate and process information effectively, allowing us to make sense of the world around us. It also enables us to recall past experiences and apply them when making decisions or solving problems. Furthermore, working memory allows us to temporarily store new information so that we can use it when needed.

Without this type of cognitive function, our ability to learn would be severely limited as we wouldn't be able to retain any new knowledge for more than a few seconds at a time. As such, working memory is an invaluable part of learning and understanding complex concepts[13].

Short-term memory is like a snapshot of

the present, allowing us to store and recall information briefly. It's the first step in our journey to encode, store, and retrieve memories - an essential part of our daily lives.

For decades, researchers have been exploring the fascinating world of short-term memory and its critical role in our lives. Unfortunately, this type of memory is limited; we can only store approximately seven pieces (+/- 2 pieces) of information at a time[14]. This means that if you are presented with more than seven things to remember, it can be difficult to recall all of them. However, understanding how short-term memory works can help us make the most of this precious resource!

Short-term memory is fleeting, typically lasting only up to 30 seconds unless rehearsed, repeated, or encoded in a way that helps recall. Still, it is necessary as a step in retaining information. However, if you don't take the time to review and repeat what you've learned, your knowledge will quickly fade away.

The manner in which information is absorbed into our short-term memory largely depends on how well we focus on it when first exposed. If something grabs our attention, then the likelihood of us being able to recall it later increases significantly. Furthermore, suppose the data has a personal connection or relevance to us. This further boosts its chances of being remembered more effectively than something lacking personal significance. This is one reason that the memory devices discussed later work so well. They help to create an emotional connection to the material.

Having a good grasp of short-term memory helps us understand how to better utilize it. Without its ability to temporarily store small amounts of data, tasks such as following directions or quickly recalling phone numbers during conversations would be impossible! Understanding how this type of memory works can help you improve your cognitive abilities and help others better understand their mental capacities too.

Implicit memory is a type of memory

that does not require conscious effort or recollection. It is the ability to remember and use information without knowing how it was acquired. Implicit memory can be divided into two categories: procedural memories, which are related to motor skills, and priming effects, which involve unconscious influences on behavior[15].

Procedural memories are formed through repeated practice or experience with a task or skill. Examples include riding a bike, playing an instrument, typing on a keyboard, and driving a car. These types of memories are stored in the brain's basal ganglia and cerebellum regions and do not require conscious recall for performance; they become automatic after enough practice.

Priming effects refer to the influence that prior experiences have on our current behavior without us being consciously aware of them. For example, if you hear someone say "apple," you may think about red apples even though no color was mentioned because you have seen red apples before in your life (a priming effect). Priming effects can also occur when we encounter words that we associate with specific emotions. If we see the word "fear" written down somewhere, it might make us feel anxious even though nothing else has happened yet (emotional priming effect). Priming effects are thought to be stored in the hippocampus region of the brain and other areas associated with emotion processing, like the amygdala[16].

Long-term memory is a type of memory that stores information for an extended period. It is the ability to remember past events, facts, and experiences.

Psychologists and neuroscientists have studied long-term memory extensively to understand how it works and how it can be improved.

The process of transferring this information into long-term storage is known as consolidation, which occurs when neurons form connections with each other to store new data. Once consolidated, this new knowledge can be retrieved from our

long-term memories
at any point in time
without having to re-
encode or reconsolidate
it again. This makes
retrieving previously
learned material much
easier than learning
something for the first
time. We don't have to
go through all the steps
involved with encoding
and consolidating again.

Long-term memories
are also more durable
than short-term
ones because they
are less likely to be
forgotten over time.
Their stronger neural
connections make
them harder to disrupt

or erase completely[17].
Additionally, these
memories tend to
become more vivid
over time as we recall
them more often and
add details based on
our current experiences

or understanding of a particular topic or event from our past.

The human brain is an incredible and mysterious organ, capable of performing complex tasks that are still largely unknown to us. As we continue to study neuroscience, we uncover more and more about the inner workings of the brain and how it functions.

With further research into this field, we can gain a better understanding of how our brains work and use this knowledge to make better use of its capabilities. We have already seen some amazing breakthroughs in neuroscience over the past few decades that have allowed us to treat neurological diseases such as Alzheimer's or Parkinson's with greater success than ever before.

We can also now understand why certain behaviors occur in people with mental health issues like depression or anxiety, which has enabled us to develop treatments for these conditions too. But there is still so much left for us to discover about the brain – from its structure and function down to its molecular level – that will help us unlock even more potential.

By continuing our studies into neuroscience, we can learn how best to optimize our brains for maximum performance in areas such as memory recall, problem-solving skills, creativity, and emotional regulation. This could lead to improved mental health and enhanced cognitive abilities across all aspects of life – from education through business management to retirement age!

The possibilities are endless when it comes to furthering our knowledge of neuroscience. Every new discovery brings with it a wealth of opportunities for improving ourselves both mentally and physically.

PART II: READ FASTER

CHUNKING

At the start of this fascinating journey, we delved into the importance of taking in chunks and reducing sub-vocalization while reading. Let's get into a little more detail so you can continue improving!

Chunking is a technique used in speed reading to increase reading speed and comprehension. The method involves breaking down the text into small chunks or groups of words rather than reading word by word. This allows the brain to process information more efficiently and quickly, as it can focus on a smaller amount of data at a time. Additionally, it makes it easier for the reader to identify patterns and themes in the text, which can help to increase understanding and retention of the material. Chunking can be applied to any type of text, from novels to technical documents. It is a powerful tool for anyone looking to improve their reading skills and increase productivity[18].

Learning to read in chunks is initially a little strange. But it's why the text is laid out in the slowly-expanding column in this book. It's there to help you get used to reading in chunks while making those chunks bigger. We are expanding your field of vision.

Expanding your field of vision is an important aspect of reading quickly. It refers to taking in more text at a glance, which can significantly increase reading speed and comprehension. By expanding your field of vision, you can process more information in less time.

One way to expand

your field of vision is to practice using your peripheral vision. To get a sense of what you can see, complete the following exercise[19]:

1. Look straight ahead and focus on a distant point.
2. Hold your two forefingers horizontally in front of you, about 30 inches from the bridge of your nose.
3. Slowly move your fingers apart while keeping your eyes focused on the distant point. Stop moving your fingers when you can no longer see their movement out of the corners of your eyes.
4. Note the distance between your fingers to determine your horizontal field of vision.
5. Repeat the exercise, this time holding your fingers vertically. Move them

apart until you can no longer see the movement out of the top and bottom of your field of vision.

6.   Note the distance between your fingers to determine your vertical field of vision.

It's incredible how large your field of vision is! We need to use this information to our advantage. We can begin to leverage it by reading at an optimal distance. According to Tony Buzan, this distance is around 20 inches when sitting in a natural position. This distance makes it easier for the eyes to focus on groups of words and reduces the likelihood of eye strain and headaches. To test this, try observing your finger close up and then observing your whole hand from a distance of about 18 inches[2].

When we read, we tend to focus on a small area of text. For many, this is one word at a time. By training yourself to use more of your peripheral vision, you can take in more text at a glance, which can significantly increase your reading speed. We are training the horizontal field of vision now! If you are still reading each line with one fixation, you have improved from where we started.

It is also important to note that expanding your field of vision is not only about how much you can see but also how much you can understand. Focusing on the meaning of what you are reading can increase your understanding and retention of the material. We will talk more about that in part three.

Another way to expand your field of vision is to practice looking at multiple lines of text in one chunk. Many expert readers can take in an entire paragraph at one glance instead of reading line by line. This allows the reader to quickly

grasp the main idea of the
text and move on to the
next section, increasing
reading speed and

comprehension[20].
When expanding
your field of vision,
it's important to find
a comfortable starting
point and gradually push
yourself to read faster. To
do this, seek out materials
you can use for practice
and experiment with
formatting the text to
increase the size of chunks
you can read with each
glance. You can do this by
cutting and pasting text
into a document, like a
Google document, then
adjusting the column
and text size to suit your
purpose. This will help
you to read faster and with
better comprehension.
By gradually pushing
your boundaries, you
will be able to increase
your reading speed
and improve your
understanding of the
material.

TEST #2

It's time to check your progress! It's the same idea as the first test, except that we will keep our current column size.

Just before you start reading, begin timing yourself. Stop your timer as soon as you are done. The reading score formula will be at the end of the reading selection. There will be ten comprehension questions and answers.

Let's begin!

Art is a medium that has been used for centuries to express emotions, thoughts, and ideas. Some art pieces have become so famous that they are recognized by people worldwide. One of the most famous art pieces in the world is the *Mona Lisa*, a painting created by Leonardo da Vinci in the early 16th century. It is a portrait of a woman with an enigmatic smile and is considered one of the greatest works of art of all time. *The Mona Lisa* is currently housed at the Louvre Museum in Paris, France.

Another famous art piece is *The Scream*, a painting created by Edvard Munch in the late 19th century. It depicts a figure standing on a bridge, screaming in terror, and is considered one of the most iconic works of art of the 19th century. It is housed at the National Museum in Oslo, Norway.

Starry Night by Vincent van Gogh is another famous art piece. Painted in 1889, it depicts a view of the village of Saint-Rémy-de-Provence at night. The painting is known for its swirling, dreamlike quality and is considered one of the greatest examples of Post-Impressionism. It is housed at the Museum of Modern Art in New York City.

The Persistence of Memory by Salvador Dali is another famous painting, created in 1931, and depicts a barren landscape with melting pocket watches draped over various objects. The painting is considered a masterpiece of Surrealism and is housed at the Museum of Modern Art in New York City.

Last but not least, *The Birth of Venus* by Sandro Botticelli is a famous painting from the 15th century that depicts the goddess Venus emerging from the sea as a fully-formed woman. It is considered one of the greatest works of art of the Renaissance period and is housed at the Uffizi Gallery in Florence, Italy.

In addition to individual art pieces, there are also several significant art movements that have had a major impact on the art world. One of the most important art movements was the Renaissance, which lasted from the 14th to the 17th century. This movement marked a shift towards realism and the use of perspective in art and produced some of the most famous and influential works of art of all time.

Another important art movement is the Baroque, which lasted from the late 16th century to the early 18th century. This movement is characterized by its grandeur, drama, and ornate decorations and is known for its emotional and theatrical qualities.

In the 19th century, Impressionism emerged as a major art movement. It is characterized by its emphasis on light and color and the use of small, visible brushstrokes. Impressionist paintings are known for their ability to capture the feeling of a moment in time and are considered some of the most beautiful works of art ever created.

In the early 20th century, Surrealism emerged as an art movement. It is characterized by its use of symbolism, dreamlike imagery, and the use of the subconscious. Surrealism is known for its ability to express the innermost thoughts and feelings of the artist, and many of the works produced by this movement are considered masterpieces.

Finally, Abstract Expressionism is another major art movement that emerged in the mid-20th century. It is characterized by its emphasis on the spontaneous and the automatic, and its focus on the process of creating art. Many of the works produced by this movement are considered some of the most important works of art of the 20th century.

Each of these art movements has played an important role in shaping the art world and has produced some of the most famous and influential works of art in history. They continue to inspire and influence artists today, and many of the techniques and styles developed during these movements are still used in art today.

Stop the timer!

To determine your current reading speed, do the following:

Divide 644 by the number of minutes it took you to read the selection.

644 words / ___ minutes = ___ wpm

That is your current reading speed.

Now, let's test your comprehension. Answer ten questions on the content of the article.

1. When was the *Mona Lisa* painted?
2. Who painted *The Scream*?
3. When was *Starry Night* painted?
4. What movement is *The Persistence of Memory* associated with?
5. Where is *The Birth of Venus* currently housed?
6. What is the Renaissance art movement?
7. What are the characteristics of Baroque art?
8. What are impressionist paintings known for?
9. What is the main purpose of Surrealism art?

10. What are the
    characteristics
    of Abstract
    Expressionism
    art?

Answers

1. The *Mona Lisa* was painted by Leonardo da Vinci in the early 16th century.
2. *The Scream* is a painting created by Edvard Munch in the late 19th century.
3. *Starry Night* is a painting created by Vincent van Gogh in 1889.
4. *The Persistence of Memory* is considered a masterpiece of Surrealism.
5. *The Birth of Venus* is currently housed at the Uffizi Gallery in Florence, Italy.
6. The Renaissance art movement marked a shift towards realism and the use of perspective in art.

7. The Baroque art movement is characterized by its grandeur, drama, and ornate decorations.

8. Impressionist paintings are known for their ability to capture the feeling of a moment in time.

9. Surrealism is known for its ability to express the innermost thoughts and feelings of the artist.

10. Abstract Expressionism is characterized by its emphasis on the spontaneous and the automatic, and its focus on the process of creating art.

Mark your score out

of /10.

SUB-VOCALIZATION AND POINTING

Earlier, we briefly talked about sub-vocalization, but now let's explore it a little further. One problem with sub-vocalization is that it slows down the reading process. When reading, the brain has to process and understand the meaning of the text, as well as keep track of where the eyes are on the page. When sub-vocalizing, the brain has the added load of mentally sounding out the words, which can slow down the reading process. This can make it difficult to read quickly and efficiently[21].

Sub-vocalization can cause fatigue and strain on the eyes

as the brain works harder to process the information. Reading can become both tiring and boring. Our inner voice slows us down and causes irrelevant thoughts, impeding comprehension. Additionally, focusing on the sound of the words can make it harder to fully understand and retain the information and hinder the ability to make connections between different pieces of information. Furthermore, sub-vocalization can lead to a lack of focus and concentration while reading, making it harder to stay engaged and interested in the material.

When reading, the brain processes information in a visual manner. Without sub-vocalization, comprehension can be enhanced as the brain is able to process the information more directly.

We can let the text stick in our minds and even create mental images. In turn, we use those images as cognitive markers, which will be discussed in more detail later. For now, when reading about a person, try to imagine what they look like, what they are wearing, and what their facial expression is. When reading about a place, try to imagine what it looks like, what the weather is like, and what the atmosphere is like. By doing this, you are creating a visual representation of the text in your mind, which can help to improve comprehension and retention.

At first, this technique might seem odd or difficult, but it will become easier with practice. The key is to be consistent and to make a conscious effort to imagine images while reading. With time, your mind will start automatically creating images while reading, and you will find that you can read faster and retain more information. It all begins by sub-vocalizing less, with the goal of eliminating the voice over time.

Also, you can use a finger or pointer to guide your focus. Using a pointer while reading improves reading speeds in several ways. Firstly, it helps to keep the eyes focused on the text and prevents them from wandering, which can slow you down. Having another physical connection to the text can help process and retain the information being read.

A pointer helps reduce the cognitive load[22]. When reading, the brain has to process and understand the meaning of the text, as well as keep track of where the eyes are on the page. Using a pointer or finger guides the eyes through the text, reducing the need for the brain to keep track of eye movement. This allows the brain to focus more on processing and understanding the text, making reading less tiring and more efficient.

When chunking text, the pointer should be placed at the middle point of the chunk to be read. Smoothly moving to the next spot can help the eye quickly locate the correct place. I personally use a pointer under the current line I am reading to help guide me. I don't move back and forth but instead use the pointer to keep me on the correct line. Regardless, find the method that works best for you. Experiment with different ways of moving across the text to improve speed and comprehension.

You can elevate your reading speeds by harnessing the power chunking, eliminating sub-vocalization, and using a pointer. These principles of speed reading can bring about incredible benefits when used together. However, to truly reap the rewards, it's essential to consistently practice these techniques for at least ten minutes each day. With dedication and perseverance, you can become a speed-reading master in no time!

A WORD ABOUT FIXATION AND RECURSION

The techniques discussed earlier are designed to address the common reading problems of fixation and recursion. Fixation occurs when a reader's eyes linger too long on one word or phrase, causing a loss of comprehension and decreased reading speed. Recursion is the act of re-reading the same words or lines multiple times, leading to a decrease in overall reading efficiency[23].

By understanding and being aware of these issues, readers can take proactive measures to avoid them. When you find yourself shuffling back to re-read the text, you must stop and figure out why it is happening.

One common reason for recursion is distraction. If a reader is easily distracted, they may find their mind wandering and have to re-read the same passage to regain their focus. Poor reading habits, such as reading too slowly or not using a pointer, can also lead to recursion.

Poor comprehension can also be a reason for recursion. If a reader has difficulty with comprehension, they may re-read passages to try to grasp the meaning. Poor memory and poor attention span can also contribute to recursion. If a reader has difficulty with memory, they may re-read passages to retain the information. If a reader has a problem with attention span, they may re-read passages to try to keep their focus on the material.

It's important to note that not all recursion is bad, and it can happen to the best readers.

Sometimes re-reading a passage is necessary to fully understand the material. However, if it becomes a pattern, it can signify that the reader needs to adjust their approach and try to improve their reading habits and skills. The answer to most recursion problems can likely be found in this book.

Fewer eye fixations result in faster reading, as the eye only takes in what it reads while at rest[24]. This means that we must pause periodically to read effectively. However, suppose we want to increase our reading speed and efficiency. In that case, we need to make fewer pauses and shorten their duration.

For example, if you stop at every word when you read a book of 60,000 words, you will have to make 60,000 pauses. If you take in two words at a time and pause for the same duration, your reading time for that book is halved!

We can drastically reduce the reading time by ingesting even more words per pause and reducing the duration. Suddenly, a novel that took five hours to finish can be read in one or two hours! This is not an impossible feat. It's achievable with practice and dedication towards improving one's eye fixations during reading.

The only way to improve the number of fixations and the time of each fixation is by being aware of it and actively working to refine your visual scanning habits. With conscious effort, you can train yourself to make fewer fixations in less time, allowing for more efficient visual processing. This training requires focus and dedication, but with enough practice, you can significantly improve your ability to quickly identify important information from a text. Additionally, this skill will not only help you process information faster but also help develop better comprehension skills as well as improved memory recall.

TEST #3

It's time to check your progress! Just before you start reading, begin timing yourself. Stop your timer as soon as you are done. The reading score formula will be at the end of the reading selection. There will be ten comprehension questions and answers.

Let's begin!

Humans have been inventing things for thousands of years, with many of the earliest known inventions dating back to ancient civilizations. From the invention of the wheel in ancient Mesopotamia to the development of paper in ancient Egypt, these early inventions greatly impacted human society and set the stage for future technological advancements.

One of the most significant early inventions was the wheel. This invention, which is believed to have originated in Mesopotamia around 3500 BCE, was used for transportation and for making pottery. The wheel greatly improved transportation and made it easier to move goods and people. It also allowed for the development of the chariot, which was used in war and transportation.

Another important invention from ancient Mesopotamia was the plow, which allowed for more efficient farming and increased food production. The invention of irrigation systems, such as the shaduf and the qanat, in ancient Egypt and Mesopotamia allowed for the cultivation of crops in areas with limited water resources.

In ancient Egypt, the invention of paper, made from papyrus, was a significant development that made it possible to record important information and preserve it for future generations. The ancient

Egyptians also invented the sundial, which was used to tell time and the hieroglyphs, a system of writing that used pictures and symbols.

During the Middle Ages, many new inventions were developed in Europe and Asia, such as the watermill, the windmill, and the mechanical clock. These inventions greatly improved efficiency in agriculture and industry, as well as allowed for more accurate timekeeping. The invention of the astrolabe, an ancient navigation tool, was also significant as it allowed sailors to navigate by the stars and determine their latitude.

After the Middle Ages, many new inventions and technological advancements were made that greatly impacted human society and shaped the modern world.

One of the most significant inventions of the 18th and 19th centuries was the steam engine, which was developed by James Watt. The steam engine greatly improved transportation and made it possible for trains and steamboats to travel at faster speeds. The invention of the cotton gin by Eli Whitney revolutionized the cotton industry and made it much more efficient. The assembly line, developed by Henry Ford, greatly increased production and made manufacturing more efficient.

In the 20th century, the invention of the telephone and radio revolutionized communication, making it possible to talk to people across the globe. The invention of the television and the computer also had a significant impact on the way we communicate and access information. The development of the internet and the World Wide Web made it possible for people to access information and communicate with each other from anywhere in the world.

In the field of medicine, many new inventions and technological advancements have been made that have greatly improved our ability to diagnose and treat illnesses.

The X-ray machine, developed by Wilhelm Roentgen, allowed for the visualization of bones and internal organs. The development of antibiotics, such as penicillin, greatly improved our ability to fight bacterial infections. The invention of the polio vaccine by Jonas Salk helped to eradicate this once-devastating disease.

In the 21st century, many new inventions and technological advancements have continued to shape the world, including the development of smartphones, social media, and the rise of artificial intelligence. The development of renewable energy sources, such as wind and solar power, has also had a significant impact on the way we produce and consume energy.

In conclusion, throughout history, inventions have played a major role in shaping the course of human civilization. From the wheel to the latest AI technologies, human curiosity and creativity have driven the development of new tools and technologies that have improved our lives in countless ways. These inventions have shaped the way we live and have laid the foundation for future technological advancements that will continue to shape the world we live in.

Stop the timer!

To determine your current reading speed, do the following:

Divide 647 by the number of minutes it took you to read the selection.

647 words / ___ minutes = ____ wpm

That is your current reading speed.

Now, let's test your comprehension. Answer ten questions on the content of the article.

1. What was the first invention mentioned in the article?
2. What did the invention of the wheel in ancient Mesopotamia allow for?

3. What was the significance of the invention of paper in ancient Egypt?
4. What was the purpose of the astrolabe?
5. During which period was the astrolabe invented?
6. What were two significant inventions of the 18th and 19th centuries?
7. How did the invention of the telephone and radio revolutionize communication?
8. What was the significance of the development of antibiotics?
9. What were two critical developments during the 21st century?
10. What were the most significant inventions in the field of medicine?

Answers:

1. The wheel was the first invention mentioned in the article.
2. The invention of the wheel allowed for improved transportation.
3. The significance of the invention of paper in ancient Egypt was that it made it possible to record important information and preserve it for future generations.
4. The astrolabe was a navigation tool. It allowed sailors to navigate by the stars.
5. The astrolabe was invented during the Middle Ages.
6. Some significant inventions of the 18th and 19th centuries were the steam engine, the cotton gin, and the assembly line.
7. The invention of the telephone and radio revolutionized

communication by making it possible to talk to people across the globe.

8. The discovery of antibiotics was significant because it greatly improved our ability to fight bacterial infections.

9. During the 21st century, advancements were made in the development of smartphones, social media, AI, and renewable energy.

10. The most significant inventions in the field of medicine were the X-ray machine, antibiotics, and the polio vaccine.

Mark your score out of   /10.

PREVIEW, QUESTION, READ, REVIEW

Previewing material before reading can be a valuable tool for improving speed, comprehension, and retention. By previewing the material, you can gain a general understanding of what the text will be about, identify key concepts and ideas, and get a sense of the structure and organization of the material. Knowing these pieces of information ahead of time will make it easier to read faster.

One of the most effective ways to preview material is to scan the headings and subheadings, as well as any bold or italicized words or phrases. These elements can often provide a quick overview of the main ideas and themes of the text. Additionally, looking at the introduction, summary, or conclusion can also give you a sense of the main points that the author is trying to convey.

Another technique for previewing material is to read the first and last sentences of each paragraph. This can give you a sense of the paragraph's main idea and how it fits into the text's overall structure[25].

Previewing material can also help you identify gaps in your knowledge or areas you may need to research further. This can be especially useful when reading technical or scholarly material, as it can help you to focus your attention on the most essential information and avoid getting bogged down in details that may not be relevant to your needs.

Asking questions before reading can effectively guide your understanding and focus your attention on the most important aspects of the text. After previewing the material, you should have a general sense of the main ideas and themes and any gaps in your knowledge[26].

One way to generate questions is to use the headings and subheadings as a starting point. For example, you might ask, "What is the main argument of this section?" or "What are the key points being made in this subsection?"

Another way to generate questions is to focus on the key concepts and ideas identified during the previewing process. For example, if you notice a specific term or phrase that is bolded or italicized, you might ask, "What is the significance of this concept?" or "How does this idea relate to the overall theme of the text?"

In addition, you can also ask questions about the structure and organization of the text. You might ask, "How is the text divided into sections?" or "What is the purpose of the introduction?"

You can also ask questions that reflect the main points of the text. "What are the major findings of this research?" or "What is the author's conclusion about the topic?"

As you read, leverage what you did during the preview to move quicker through the text. Utilize the questions you formulated to concentrate on the most pertinent details, but be open to revising or expanding your list of questions as necessary to better understand the material.

Finally, it's crucial to review the information that you've read. This step will help solidify your understanding of the material and retain the information to stay in your long-term memory. Reviewing can be done in a variety of ways. One way is to summarize the key points in your own words. Another is to create flashcards or visual aids to help you remember important details. You could also practice retrieval by testing yourself on the information you've learned. You can also review the material with someone else, whether discussing it with a study partner or teaching it to someone else. This can help reinforce your understanding and identify areas where you may need to spend more time studying.

By using a comprehensive approach that includes previewing, questioning, reading, and reviewing material, you can establish a strong foundation for retaining and remembering the information from any text you read. This approach allows you to understand the main ideas and themes, focus on the most important details, and solidify your knowledge of the material through review and practice.

PART III: REMEMBER MORE

IMPROVE CONCENTRATION, IMPROVE LEARNING

Distraction is one of the biggest obstacles to effective learning. When we are distracted, our attention is pulled away from the task at hand, making it difficult to focus and absorb new information.

Right now, are there things that are taking away your focus? Is the television on? Is your phone next to you, buzzing and beeping with notifications? Is there music playing in the background?

And what about your mind? Is it clear, or are you thinking about other things? Is some distracting thought nagging at you? Internal distractions can be harder to fix because we can't just turn them off like a television.

To fully absorb and remember what we read, we need complete concentration, especially if we want to ramp up our reading speeds. If we're not paying attention, we'll have to review the material repeatedly before it finally sinks in, which is a waste of time.

Even though it's mentioned often, it's worth noting that a good night's sleep is critical for concentration, memory, and learning. If we want to perform at our best, we must sleep[27].

Even after a good night's sleep, it can be hard to keep our minds focused. There are many reasons why our minds might wander. But with this list of anti-distraction techniques, we can learn to focus.

Purpose

In *The Power of Unwavering Focus*, Dandapani says that the most important thing we can do when seeking focus is to find the purpose behind what we're doing[28]. A clear purpose provides motivation.

For example, consider why you

want to read faster. Is it to learn more? Maybe you're struggling with too much reading in the workplace or a college class. Or perhaps you just want to read a hundred books this year.

There are many reasons why someone might want to read faster. Once you're clear about your purpose, it's easier to focus because your mind wants to achieve cognitive consonance[4]. Your brain wants your actions, behaviors, and values to be aligned, and determining the importance of something will make your mind pay attention.

Illumination

Imagine that you have a flashlight in your mind. This flashlight will cast a small circle of light on just one thing in your mind. Right now, use the flashlight to see a past event. Make it a pleasant memory, like a family gathering, a walk outside, or anything else you choose. See the memory in a circle of light, with everything else around it being dark. Move closer to the memory until it fills your field of vision.

Make this event big and colorful in your mind. Try to visualize the people and the scenery. Can you recall the smell? What did you hear? Did something significant happen? Was it fun or relaxing? How did this event make you feel?

Once you've explored the memory, step back. Leave the scene and watch it get smaller. Turn off the flashlight and let the memory fade into darkness for now.

We can use this flashlight tool to help us focus our attention[29]. When we focus on just one thing at a time, we mentally block out other irrelevant thoughts. Anytime we need to focus on something, we can imagine this flashlight shining on a specific topic.

Try it now. Imagine that a small circle of light is shining on this page. Everything outside the illuminated spot falls into darkness and is currently irrelevant. Step closer to the light and let the text fill your field of vision. Notice how focused you are on the words that you are reading.

As long as the light shines, it's

almost impossible for the mind to wander. It's a great tool you can use anytime you need to pay full attention.

Take Breaks

Even when we're engaged in something we find moderately interesting, our concentration tends to wane after a while. Sometimes, we can bring ourselves back to attention, but when we can't, it's time to take a break. According to John Medina, some people become too distracted to work after just ten minutes[30].

Even when we use strategies to refocus and concentrate, taking quick breaks to give our minds a rest is much more effective than long cramming sessions. Taking a few minutes to do some light physical activity, like going for a walk, can help reset our minds and allow us to return to our tasks with renewed focus. Breaks are an important part of maintaining concentration and preventing mental fatigue. So next time you find your attention flagging, consider taking a short break to refresh your mind and return to your work with renewed energy and focus.

Decide to Concentrate

As Tony Robbins points out, our brains and bodies always follow through on true decisions[31]. In other words, if we genuinely decide to do something, we will do it. This principle applies not only to life-altering resolutions but to smaller choices as well.

Sometimes, all it takes to regain focus is a loud inner thought, a decision to concentrate. If we give ourselves a command, our minds strive for unity and will work to follow through on it. By using your sternest inner voice and telling yourself, "I am going to give this project my complete attention right now," you can take control of your focus and get things done.

So next time you find yourself losing focus, try making a genuine decision to concentrate. Use your inner voice to give yourself a command, and watch as your brain and body follow through. With practice, you'll find it easier and easier to regain and maintain your focus.

Use Mental Balloons

"You had to live—did live, from habit that became instinct—in the assumption that every sound you made was overheard by social media, and, except in darkness do laundry, every moment scrutinized by social media. I had better hop on Instagram and do the laundry."

Wait. What just happened?

The quote is mostly from one of my favorite novels, *Nineteen Eighty-Four*, by George Orwell, but with a few interruptions from my mind. Isn't that how it starts? The mind begins to insert thoughts into the text without the reader knowing it happened. Soon, the eyes are still moving over the text, but no one is reading anymore. Instead, the reader is thinking about other things.

If you find yourself losing focus, here is a quick fix that can help. It's called the mental balloon technique. I have no idea where it comes from, but here's how it works:

1. Stop reading for a moment.

2. Mentally inflate a giant red balloon.
3. Stuff the distracting thought inside the balloon. It doesn't matter what form the thought takes – whether it's text, audio, or images – just stuff it inside the balloon.
4. Watch the thought-stuffed balloon float away. Keep watching until it turns into a speck in the distance.

For some reason, this process stops the intrusive thought from returning for a while, giving you time to refocus on your work. Try it next time you find your mind wandering, and see if it helps.

Don't Multitask

Reading a book? Check. Writing an essay at the same time? Double check. Looking at social media while doing those two things? Triple check. Youtube tab open and playing something in the background? Quadruple check.

The belief that humans can multitask is widespread, and it is often thought to be based on the idea that the brain is similar to a computer capable of multitasking[32]. However, this belief is not well-supported by scientific evidence. In fact, research has shown that the human brain is not well-suited for multitasking, and attempting to multitask can decrease productivity and increase the risk of errors.

One reason people may cling to the belief that humans can multitask is that they have experienced situations where they have been able to perform multiple tasks at once, such as talking on the phone while driving or responding to emails while watching TV. However, these tasks do not require complex cognitive processing and can be performed automatically without much conscious effort. But even these simple tasks aren't being done to the best of our abilities.

In contrast, tasks that require more cognitive processing, such as reading, writing, or solving a math problem, are more difficult to multitask. When we try to perform these tasks simultaneously, our brain must constantly switch back and forth between them, which can be mentally exhausting and lead to a decrease in performance.

When it comes to multitasking, it is a myth that we are capable of it. Instead, we can only context switch between tasks, leading to decreased concentration, memory, and productivity. A study by the University of California found that multitasking can also lead to increased anxiety, impaired creative thinking, and more mistakes in our work. Additionally, multitasking prevents us from achieving a state of flow, which is necessary for performing at our best. Research has shown that it can take over nine minutes to fully immerse ourselves in a new task after switching from another job. This indicates we are wasting valuable time and energy trying to juggle multiple tasks simultaneously. Instead, it is better to focus on one task at a time to achieve the best results[33].

Contrary to popular belief, what we call multitasking is actually context-switching. This can be a time-wasting and inefficient process, particularly if the tasks require different skill sets or require the brain to switch between different contexts[34].

For example, if you were working on math homework for a few minutes and then shifted to essay writing, it could take over nine minutes for your brain to fully become immersed in the new task and achieve optimal performance. This is because the brain must first adjust to the new context and task demands, which can be mentally exhausting and lead to decreased productivity.

Additionally, constantly switching between tasks can lead to a higher risk of error as the brain is not entirely focused on any one task. Concentrating on one task at a time is often more effective than attempting to multitask or context switch. By completing one task before moving on to the next, we can avoid the time and productivity losses associated with context switching and achieve better overall performance.

The more tasks we attempt to switch between, the more

our productivity suffers. To demonstrate this, try the following exercise:

1. Get a lined sheet of paper and a pen or pencil.
2. Have someone time you as you complete the following task: On the first line, write, "I am a great multitasker." On the second line, write out the numbers 1-20 sequentially. This task typically takes about twenty seconds.

Now, try the same thing in a "multitasking" style:

1. Skip a few lines on the sheet of paper.
2. Again, have someone time you as you complete the next part.
3. Write the same two lines as in the first test (I am a great multitasker on line one and the numbers 1-20 on line two), except this time, write one letter on one line and then a number on the line below it.

For example, write "I" on the first line and the number "1" below it.

Next, go to the first line and write "a" followed by "2" below it. Continue until you have completed both lines.

You will likely find that completing the second version of this activity takes longer as your brain must constantly switch between the two lines and the different types of information being written. This demonstrates how attempting to multitask, or context switch can negatively impact productivity.

It won't take long to realize that attempting to multitask can lead to slower performance and a higher risk of errors. Every time you switch between tasks, it takes a moment for your brain to reset and figure out what is next. This can be mentally exhausting and lead to decreased productivity. When the nature of the task changes, it takes longer for our minds to switch to the new challenge and perform at optimal levels.

This is why focusing on one task at a time is better. Working on one job will help you become more attentive, accurate, and productive. If you want to improve your focus and productivity, this is the most important suggestion to follow. By focusing on one task at a time, you can avoid the negative consequences of multitasking and context switching and achieve better overall performance.

Eliminate Distractions

To improve your ability to concentrate, you should eliminate environmental distractions before starting work. This means closing your laptop, putting your phone in another room, and turning off the TV. Even music with lyrics can hinder your concentration. So, classical music without lyrics is a good option if you require some background noise. If you can't control the environment, try using headphones to block out noise.

To create a productive workspace, sit in a straight-back chair. Sit at a desk or table. This helps to make your work environment look more professional and conducive to productivity[35]. If it's impossible to create a space like this, don't worry – the other concentration tips will still be effective even in a less-than-ideal working environment.

Sliders for Attention

Have you heard of neuro-linguistic programming (NLP)? It's a type of psychotherapy that uses tools like visualization to make changes and is claimed to be able to treat issues such as phobias and depression with just one treatment.

While I am generally skeptical of NLP, and some of the claims made by practitioners can be extreme, I find that one technique – using mental sliders to increase and decrease the intensity of a particular feeling – can effectively improve concentration. The following trick is one that Paul McKenna describes[36].

Imagine that you have a knob on the left side of your forehead that you can slide back and forth. On the left side of the slider is passive concentration, and on the right is active concentration.

1. Start by sliding the knob to your left and thinking about a time when you passively concentrated on something,

like watching a TV show or listening to music while relaxing. You didn't need to put in much effort or focus, but you were still paying attention.

2. Try to recreate the feeling of that moment in your mind. See what you saw, hear what you heard, and feel how relaxed and passive you were while absorbing the information. Remember, the knob is on the left.

3. Repeat the process of sliding the knob to the left and re-experiencing that moment at least three more times.

4. Now, slide the knob to the right and think about a time when you were fully engaged and actively concentrating on your work. You had plenty of energy and were working as much as possible. If you can't think of a specific time, make one up in your mind. Imagine yourself in a state of pure concentration, or "flow."

5. Re-live that moment in your

mind, making the scene as big and colorful as possible. See it, hear it, and feel it.

6. Repeat the process of sliding the knob to the right and re-experiencing the memory at least three more times. Each time, make sure the knob is on the right.

7. Gently slide the knob back to the left and think about another time when you were relaxed and passively concentrating.

8. Gently slide the knob to the right and think about another time when you were in a state of active concentration or "flow." If you can't think of another time, create a second scene in your mind where you are in a flow state.

9. Repeat the process of sliding the knob left while thinking about moments of passive focus and sliding it right while replaying scenes of active concentration at least three more times.

10. When you're finished, slide

the knob all the way to the
left.

11. Slowly move the knob
towards the middle,
noticing how your
concentration increases
as you go. When you
reach the center, take a
moment to notice that
you feel halfway between
relaxed focus and active
concentration.

12. Continue sliding the knob
to the right, still noticing
the increase in focus.

13. When the knob is all the
way to the right, take note
of how fully engaged and
focused you feel.

14. Slowly slide the knob back
to the left, noticing how
your concentration eases
up.

That's it.

Depending on your needs, you can
use the slider technique to dial in
your focus. Over the next few weeks,
try reinforcing the link between
passive focus on the left and
active concentration on the right by

adding moments of each to your daily routine. This technique can be very effective in improving focus.

These quick-fix strategies can help you get more out of your study periods. Use any combination of them to boost your focus and productivity. Through repeated effort, you will also find that you can get into a state of focus easier and for a longer period of time. Even though they are quick fixes, they should help develop better concentration over the long term. I hope you find them as helpful as I have over the years.

ORGANIZING INFORMATION

Organizing information into manageable wedges is a handy tool for anyone who needs to remember complex facts or data.

With wedging, we can take big ideas and break them down into smaller pieces that are easier to understand and recall. Wedging helps us make sense of the world around us by organizing our thoughts in a way that makes it easier for our brains to process and store information. By breaking things down into smaller parts, we can better comprehend and retain what we're learning for longer periods.

The beauty of wedging is that it doesn't just apply to memorizing facts or data; it also works with creative tasks like writing stories or designing projects. When faced with a daunting task, try breaking it up into small wedges, so you don't feel overwhelmed by the whole thing at once. This will help you stay focused on one step at a time until you reach your goal!

It is also a powerful tool for improving recall and comprehension. Breaking down large amounts of information into smaller, more manageable pieces makes remembering and processing the material more accessible. This technique can be used in many different ways, from memorizing facts to understanding complex concepts.

To wedge information, follow these steps:

1. Identify the main idea or topic of the information. This step aids in understanding and comprehending what you are reading. It requires careful analysis and critical thinking to determine what the material is about. Once you have identified the main idea, it can be broken down into smaller wedges which will help you better understand how all the

pieces fit together. This process can also help identify any key points that should be focused on when studying or discussing a particular topic.

2. Breaking down complex information into smaller, more manageable wedges is essential in the learning process. Not only does it help learners to focus on one topic at a time, but it also allows them to group related topics together for better comprehension and organization. Additionally, breaking up the material into smaller sections can make it easier to identify key points and concepts quickly. By dividing the material into bite-sized pieces, learners can recall what they have learned more easily when needed.

3. Label each wedge with a descriptive heading that summarizes its content. Each wedge needs to be accurately described so you can quickly identify what each section is about without having to read through it in detail first.

4. Organizing and grouping related wedges of information into bigger categories are essential to ensure your material is easy to comprehend

and navigate. This can be especially useful when there are multiple topics within the document, as it allows for better clarity when revisiting them later.

For instance, if you have a document that covers different aspects of history, such as politics, economics, culture, etc., these could be broken up into distinct sections or subsections for more straightforward navigation. Furthermore, each wedge should contain only relevant information so you can quickly find what you need without sifting through unrelated topics. Properly organizing your material into larger categories and subcategories will make it simpler to locate the required information while providing a more organized structure overall.

5. Review your work to ensure that all facts and figures are accurate and that the overall message of the material being wedged is clear. This means double-checking any sources you have used for accuracy, ensuring that any data or statistics are up-to-date and relevant. If any complex concepts or ideas are included in

your work, explain them clearly. Finally, read through your entire piece one more time to make sure everything flows logically from start to finish.

Wedging can be done in a variety of ways, such as grouping related items together or creating mental connections between individual pieces of information. For example, a person trying to learn a new language can group related vocabulary words together, such as *book, page,* and *pen,* to form a wedge of related words. Similarly, a musician can group musical notes together to form a chord, making it easier to recall and play.

Additionally, wedging can be achieved by creating mental connections between individual pieces of information. Imagine trying to memorize a list of grocery items. It would be much more challenging to remember the list if it were presented as a random string of things such as *milk, eggs, bread, cheese, apples,* and *chicken.* However, if you group the items together based on their category, such as *Dairy: milk, cheese; Meat: chicken; Bakery: bread;*

Produce: apples, and *eggs,* it becomes much more manageable and easy to recall.

A great example of wedging in action is the process of learning to play a piece of music on a musical instrument. When a musician first starts to learn new music, they may struggle to remember the individual notes and timing of the piece. However, as they practice and familiarize themselves with it, they begin to group the notes into wedges or phrases.

The musician may also use other techniques, such as grouping the notes based on their position on the instrument or grouping notes by their rhythm. This allows the musician to focus on one aspect of the piece at a time rather than trying to take in the entire score all at once.

As the musician continues to practice, they will begin to group more extensive wedges of the piece together, until they can play the entire song from memory. The musician will also group the song with other music they already know and create a mental map of the different pieces. This helps them to recall the songs they learned faster and easier.

This example illustrates how wedges allow the musician to take a large, complex task (learning a new piece of music) and break it down into smaller, more manageable wedges. By grouping the notes and phrases together, the musician can focus on one aspect of the piece at a time, making it easier to remember and recall the entire song.

Wedging effectively improves reading speed and comprehension by breaking text into smaller, more manageable units. It helps readers to focus on a smaller section of text at a time, which can help to reduce cognitive overload and make the reading process more efficient.

When reading a non-fiction book, a reader can group related concepts or ideas together to form a wedge of information. This allows the reader to understand the book's overall structure instead of individual pieces of information. For example, when reading a book on a particular historical event, a reader can group related information, such as the key players, the timeline of events, and the significance of the event. By doing so, the reader can understand the context and importance of the event rather than just memorizing a list of facts.

Readers can use other techniques, such as creating mental connections between the information they are reading and information they already know. This can help readers to better understand and remember the information. Suppose the text is about a historical event that parallels current news. In that case, the reader can make a mental connection between the two, which will help them to understand and remember the information better.

In today's fast-paced, information-heavy world, it's more important than ever to have efficient memory strategies to help us remember important information. That's where the technique of wedging comes in. It can help overcome short-term memory limitations by breaking large amounts of data into smaller, more manageable units, making it easier to remember and recall.

In conclusion, wedging can be a powerful tool to help overcome the limitations of short-term memory and improve the ability to remember large amounts of information. By breaking the text into smaller, more manageable units, readers can better understand and remember the information, improving memory and recall ability.

IMAGINATION AND VISUAL THINKING

Imagination and visual thinking are powerful allies in the pursuit of knowledge and understanding. Through the creative power of imagination, our minds are able to form unique mental images, concepts, and ideas that are not limited by our immediate sensory experiences. With the ability to think visually, we can take in and comprehend information more effectively through the use of pictures, diagrams, and other visual tools. Together, they enable us to create, process, and store data in our memories more effectively, making more informed decisions and gaining a deeper understanding of the world around us[37].

By creating vivid mental images of something, we can comprehend and retain it more effectively. Likewise, by forming visual cues, we can recall information stored in our minds more quickly. Such a skill can be invaluable in the pursuit of knowledge and success.

Imagination and visual thinking can be powerful tools for helping us to remember abstract concepts like numbers, dates, and names. By forming mental images or graphical representations of these ideas, we can better comprehend them and make them more memorable[38]. We'll investigate specific strategies to do that in the mnemonic devices section.

Moreover, combining creative visualization and learning can help to boost engagement, enthusiasm, and comprehension. It enables learners to link new information to their existing knowledge base, past experiences, and feelings, making it easier for them to retain.

Imagination gives us the power to conjure up vivid mental images of our daily experiences. These snapshots of information are like a personal library that we can turn to whenever we need to recall something - like a new acquaintance's name. Visualizing this person and creating an image in your mind's eye makes it easier to remember them when you meet again.

Creating mental images is a compelling way to enhance our memory retention. These unique representations of information make it easier for us to recall, and they also have strong emotional connections that further embed the memories in our minds[39]. This means we can access the information more readily and with greater accuracy than if we had simply tried to memorize it without forming a mental image. With this technique, we can use our imaginations to create vivid and lasting memories.

Unleashing the power of imagination as a mnemonic tool can be a game-changer for your memory. Imagine being able to craft unforgettable and one-of-a-kind mental images of information, effortlessly recalling them at will. Not only that but harnessing the emotional power of these mental images makes them even more ingrained in your memory. And with the added bonus of connecting new information to your existing knowledge, personal experiences, and emotions, the information becomes even more memorable and meaningful. Unleashing the power of imagination as a mnemonic tool can take your memory to new heights.

Memory is a fascinating and intricate process, and it's no secret that the brain is wired to process and understand visual information more efficiently. Studies have shown that people tend to remember things better when they have a visual representation of the data. The brain is wired to process and understand visual information more efficiently. In fact, it has been found that people can remember up to 65% more information when it is presented to them in a visual format[11]. This means that incorporating visual elements in the information we want to remember can significantly enhance our ability to recall it later.

One of the reasons why visual memory is so powerful is because it taps into the brain's natural tendency to think in pictures. The brain is wired to process visual information more quickly and efficiently than other types of information. This is because visual information is more easily processed by the brain's primary visual cortex, which is responsible for processing visual information from the eyes. These mental images are often more vivid and memorable than words alone. Additionally, images often have strong emotional connections, making them even more special.

Visual memory allows us to relate new information to our existing knowledge, personal experiences, and emotions. This helps to create a deeper understanding of the information, making it more meaningful and easier to recall.

Visual cues are a great tool when it comes to recalling information. By creating visual representations of the information, we can make unique and memorable cues to help us identify the information later. For example, mentally creating a visual map of a city can help you remember the different landmarks, streets, and other points of interest. This is because creating a visual map allows you to see the city layout in your mind and relate it to your prior experiences. Similarly, creating a visual timeline of historical events can help you remember the order in which they occurred. This is because the visual representation of events in chronological order helps to create a clear mental picture of the sequence of events, making it more memorable.

Another great use of visual cues is for memorizing lists of items. Visual cues, such as images or symbols, can help organize the information in our minds and make it more memorable. For example, using images to represent different items on a shopping list can make it easier to remember.

While reading, it is a great strategy to try and visualize these things instead of sub-vocalizing the words to yourself. The auditory cues vanish and don't have the same "sticky" characteristic as images.

Unleashing the power of imagination and visual thinking can be an incredibly effective way to improve memory and recall. There are several techniques that can be used to combine these two powerful tools to make the information more memorable.

One such technique is to create a mental image of the information and then add details to it. For example, imagine a person's face and then add labels with their name, occupation, and other relevant information. This technique allows you to create a unique and memorable mental image of the person, making it easier to recall later on.

Another powerful technique is creating a visual representation of the information and then using imagination to add context and meaning. For example, creating a visual timeline of historical events and then imagining yourself in those events will improve memory. This technique allows you to relate the historical events to your personal experiences, making them more meaningful and easier to recall.

You can also combine both techniques by creating a mental image and adding visual cues. For example, imagine walking through a city and then adding labels with the name of different landmarks, streets, and points of interest. This technique allows you to see the city layout in your mind, relate it to your prior experiences, and add labels to remember it better.

Incorporating imagination and visual thinking into your memory techniques can also be a fun and engaging way to learn and remember new information. You can make the information more exciting and memorable by using your imagination to create vivid mental images and visual representations.

Use your imagination to visualize the following text:

Once upon a time, in the lush green jungles of Africa, there lived a mighty lion named Leo. Leo was the king of the jungle, feared and respected by all the other animals. He had a magnificent mane of golden hair that flowed down his back and a roar that could be heard for miles.

Leo spent his days lounging in the sun, hunting for food, and keeping a watchful eye over his kingdom. He was a fierce hunter, feared by all the other animals, and he always led his pride on successful hunts.

One day, as Leo was out on a hunt, he came across a new animal in his jungle. It was a strange creature, unlike anything he had ever seen before. It was small and furry, with big round ears and a long bushy tail. Leo was curious and decided to follow the creature, keeping a safe distance.

The creature led Leo deep into

the jungle, to a hidden meadow surrounded by tall trees. The meadow was filled with all kinds of exotic plants and colorful flowers. Leo had never seen anything like it before. It was a peaceful and serene place. The creature turned to Leo and said, "I am the guardian of this meadow; it is a place of magic and wonder. I bring you here as a gift to enjoy its beauty and live in peace."

Leo was touched by the creature's kindness and decided to make the meadow his new home. He spent his days lounging in the sun, surrounded by the beauty of nature. He still hunted for food, but only when necessary, and he lived in harmony with all the other animals.

The meadow became a sanctuary for all the animals in the jungle, and Leo, the mighty lion, was no longer feared but loved and respected as the protector of this magical place. He ruled his kingdom with wisdom and kindness, and all the animals lived in peace and prosperity.

From that day on, the jungle was a place of wonder and beauty, and Leo, the lion king, was loved by all.

Okay, not a great story, but the ability to visualize and remember the details of a story is a powerful tool that can be applied to all aspects of learning and memory.

When we actively engage with the material, whether it's a story or any other type of information, we can create mental images that are more memorable and easier to recall. With time and practice, you'll notice a significant improvement in memory retention and recall.

MNEMONIC TECHNIQUES

Mnemonic devices are like secret superpowers for your memory! They come in different shapes and forms, like acrostics and acronyms. Think about it, with just a simple phrase like "Every Good Boy Deserves Fun" you can easily remember the notes on the lines of a treble staff in music. Acronyms are another way to boost your memory, like using "HOMES" to recall the names of the Great Lakes - Huron, Ontario, Michigan, Erie, and Superior. Trigonometry can be tricky, but with the help of an acronym like "SOH CAH TOA," you can easily remember the definitions for sine, cosine, and tangent. Embrace the power of mnemonics and watch your memory soar!

One reason for using memory techniques is to blast through the 7 +/- 2 rule, also known as Miller's Law. This cognitive psychology principle states that the average person can only hold 7 (plus or minus 2) items in their short-term memory at a time[40]. If you try to remember a list of more than 7 items, you'll have difficulty keeping them all in your head. This can be a problem when retaining large amounts of information, such as a long list of items or a complex text.

The concept of the 7 +/- 2 rule was first proposed by psychologist George Miller in 1956 in his influential paper "The Magical Number Seven, Plus or Minus Two: Some Limits on Our Capacity for Processing Information[12]." Miller's research found that people can remember 7 (plus or minus 2) items in short-term memory.

It's important to note that the 7 +/- 2 rule is just an average, and some people may have a higher or lower capacity for holding items in their short-term memory. Furthermore, the rule applies to the number of things, not the size of the information. For instance, a phone number could be considered as either seven items if taken in as individual digits or as one item if using a powerful mnemonic technique, like the Major system. We will learn how to use the

Major system in a few moments.

Before the invention of written language, remembering and recalling information was crucial for survival. This is reflected in the culture of ancient Greece, where memory was highly valued and even had its own goddess, Mnemosyne. Mnemosyne was a Titaness and the daughter of Gaia and Uranus. She was responsible for overseeing the River of Forgetting and the Pool of Remembrance in the Underworld. She was believed to have the power to grant eloquent speech to kings and poets, making her an influential figure in the world of storytelling.

The ancient Greek poets would often invoke Mnemosyne at the beginning of their tales, seeking her assistance in accurately narrating their stories. They believed that by calling upon her, she would bless them with the ability to remember and recall every detail of their stories, ensuring their audience would be captivated and enchanted by their words. Mnemosyne was not only a goddess of memory but also of eloquence and storytelling.

It is interesting to note that the word "mnemonic" itself is derived from Mnemosyne, highlighting the importance of memory in ancient Greek culture and its lasting impact on modern language. This highlights the timeless essence of memory and the various ways in which it has been revered throughout history.

Storytellers were not only entertainers but also a vital source of education and information for the younger generation. They were responsible for passing down important cultural and historical knowledge through storytelling. To fulfill this role effectively, they had to master the skill of memorization.

In ancient cultures, storytellers were trained in the art of memory from a young age. They were taught various techniques to help them remember long and complex stories, as well as historical events and customs. Although the exact methods used by these storytellers are not known, there are hints in the stories that have been passed down through the generations.

For example, in many traditional tales, you can use mnemonic devices such as repetition, rhyme, and alliteration, which were likely used to help the storytellers remember the legends. They would also use vivid imagery, similes, and metaphors to make the stories more memorable. These techniques enabled the storytellers to remember their stories and made them more engaging and captivating for the audiences.

A common technique used in oral storytelling was the association of specific adjectives with characters to aid in memory recall. For example, the character of Hercules might consistently be described as "mighty" in the story, even when he is not performing any awe-inspiring feats. Similarly, the character of Aphrodite might be described as "beautiful," even when she is committing a terrible deed. This technique helped the storyteller to easily remember which character was driving the action in the story[41].

Using these adjectives consistently, the storyteller created mental images and "mind movies" that made storing and recalling the story easier. These contextual clues provided by the adjectives helped the storyteller remember the account with greater accuracy, which was crucial in the oral tradition where there was no written record.

In ancient Greece and Rome, politicians were expected to be skilled at public speaking and have a vast reservoir of knowledge at their disposal. They were often required to impress their peers and demonstrate their expertise in order to gain an edge in their pursuit of power. To achieve this, they needed to have an extraordinary ability to recall vast amounts of information, often in the form of long lists of data points.

Politicians of ancient Greece and Rome employed various memory techniques to enhance their memory. Some of these techniques are still in use today. The politicians would hire famous rhetoricians such as Gorgias of Leontinoi and Marcus Fabius Quintilianus to help them improve their oratorical skills and acquire the art of memory. These experts in rhetoric would teach them techniques such as association, visualization, and repetition, to help them remember the information they needed to recall[42].

These ancient politicians were true masters of memory, using their skills to gain an advantage in their positions of power. They would use any information they could remember to persuade others, making them a formidable force in the political arena. The techniques used by these ancient politicians have been modified over the centuries. Still, their legacy lives on as a testament to the power of memory and the impact it can have on one's ability to achieve success.

We will look at three different memory techniques: the linking method, memory palaces, and the Major system. These techniques can be used to create vivid, unforgettable stories about anything that needs to be remembered. Each of these techniques serves a specific purpose. The linking method helps create memorable images, memory palaces leverage the brain's ability to use locations as points of recollection, and the Major system provides an easy way to remember and recall numbers.

Before we get into these techniques, here's a quick test to assess your current memory and recall abilities. Most people can remember around seven items when asked to memorize a list.

Instructions

1. Take one minute to read through the list a few times.
2. Do something else for one or two minutes. Watch a video of kittens playing, run around, or any other activity of your choice. It doesn't matter what you do, as long as you

take a short break.

3. After taking a break, put your memory to the test by trying to recreate the list as accurately as possible on a piece of paper or in your mind. Take note of how many items you can remember. If you can recall more than seven items and have them in the correct order, give yourself a pat on the back!

This simple exercise will give you an insight into your current memory and recall abilities. It will serve as a benchmark for measuring your progress as you work on enhancing your memory with the techniques discussed. It's a great way to evaluate your memory and track your progress as you continue to improve and refine your skills.

The List:

1. Comb
2. Ice cream
3. Avocado
4. Toilet paper
5. Hotdog buns
6. Toothpaste
7. Orange juice
8. French fries
9. Chicken

10.   Dish soap

Did the memory test go well?

If you recalled all ten items, that is impressive! Scoring between five and nine items is considered normal for this test. Keep in mind that short-term memory can hold an average of 7 +/- 2 pieces of information. With practice and memory techniques, anyone can achieve a score of 10/10.

Linking

The linking method, also known as association, is an effective technique for remembering all the items on the list. This system uses imagination to connect each item with the next one, creating a story with the things that need to be remembered. It's a simple yet powerful tool that can help improve memory with any type of information.

Association is the backbone of memory; everything we learn is connected to the information we already know in some way43. Psychologists have discovered that our knowledge is organized like a spider web, with new details being connected to prior knowledge. Your mind is constantly creating connections between different pieces of information, and these associations can act as a trigger for memories. Even when faced with complex math formulas or abstract concepts, association can help recall the desired information. Think of it as a mental treasure map, leading you to the information you seek, hidden deep within the depths of your mind. So, next time you need to recall something, try to think of the associations that might help you remember. It's like a secret key to unlock the vault of your memory.

Here's an example of how to use the linking method with the list provided above:

I imagine myself combing my hair, which is covered in ice cream. Whenever I lift the comb out of my hair, globs of ice cream fall to the floor and pile up into a heap of avocados. I then pick up the avocados, wrap them in toilet paper, and place them into a hot dog bun. I add toothpaste as a condiment and pour a glass of orange juice while deep-frying a French mime. Finally, I stuff all these strange items into a chicken (either alive or dead, depending on your preference) and wash it down with dish soap. This bizarre and humorous image can be used to help remember the items on the list in the correct order.

That's an image I won't forget anytime soon! It's weird and (to me, at least) funny. Humorous imagery can help make information more memorable. However, if these examples don't work for you, it's good to personalize them to make them stick.

In general, the stranger, funnier, and more bizarre our associations, the more memorable the list is. At first, it may seem easier to use pre-made stories, but with practice, you'll find it just as easy to create your own. To help you remember the key elements of effective linking, you can use the acronym SAME: Substitution, Absurdity, Movement, and Exaggeration. These elements can help make your associations more vivid and memorable.

1. Substitute

Making associations more complex can actually strengthen our memories. To remember specific words that may be difficult to visualize, using substitution or cues can be helpful. For instance, to recall the phrase "cues might help," we could substitute the word "cue" with an image of a pool cue. This doesn't mean we literally mean a pool cue, but it helps us visualize the word better. The above example uses the substitution of deep frying a French mime instead of French fries to make the image more memorable. This technique incorporates the principles of SAME: substitution, absurdity, exaggeration, and movement. The idea of a screaming, agony-stricken mime is more effective for remembering French fries than the abstract word "fries" alone.

2. Absurdity

The more absurd and outrageous the association, the better it will stick in your memory. When creating associations, you can imagine whatever you find interesting or amusing. Some people find that sex and violence are effective for reinforcing memories, while others prefer silly and funny associations. Whatever interests you is what you should use to help support your memories.

We tend to recall the most interesting, unusual, and bizarre events from the past rather than the mundane details of our everyday lives. By using your brain's natural inclination towards anything novel, you can create more effective associations for improving your memory.

3. Movement

A static image can be helpful for memory, but adding motion can make it even more effective. The more your associations resemble a mini-movie, the easier it will be to remember the items and their order. Adding action to your associations allows you to search your memory forward and backward to retrieve memories more easily. This is because our brains are wired to pay more attention to motion, even when it only happens in our minds.

One way to add motion to your associations is to imagine the objects in your list interacting with each other in a scene or story. For example, instead of simply picturing a chicken holding a hot dog bun stuffed with avocados wrapped in toilet paper, you could imagine the chicken chasing the hot dog bun around a room, with the avocados and toilet paper falling out and causing chaos as they go. This added motion can make the image more dynamic and memorable.

4. Exaggeration

Exaggerating the details in your associations can make them easier to remember. Instead of combing your hair with a regular-sized comb, you could picture yourself using a giant comb to remove huge, absurd globs of ice cream from your hair. Make the avocado piles so tall that they tower over you. The more ridiculous and over-the-top the image, the more memorable it will be.

Exaggeration can also be used to enhance other elements of your associations. For example, you could exaggerate the movement in your mini-movie by thinking about a giant cooked chicken chasing the bun or the French mime fry in the deep fryer with exaggerated facial expressions of terror. These excessive details can make the image more vivid and memorable.

Using your imagination and creativity when linking items together can make it easier to remember anything. Even memorizing math formulas can benefit from association. Using "vampires explode while biting hippies" to recall "$V = bh$" makes it more visual and memorable. Furthermore, when we create these associations, we can combine them with other techniques to make ideas even stickier. In particular, memory palaces work well with the linking method to provide long-lasting memories.

The Memory Palace

The memory palace technique, also known as the method of loci, is a powerful mnemonic device that utilizes the innate spatial memory of the brain to aid in recall. This technique involves creating a vivid mental image of a familiar place, such as a house or palace, and associating different items or information with specific locations. This method is believed to have originated in hunter-gatherer societies as a way to navigate and remember the site of resources. Still, it was popularized by the ancient Greek poet Simonides of Ceos. According to legend, by using the memory palace technique, Simonides was able to recall the names of all the guests at a banquet, even after they were killed in a tragic building collapse.

This technique is still widely used today and is an effective way to remember and organize large amounts of information. It can be used for a wide range of purposes, from studying for exams and memorizing speeches to remembering grocery lists. The technique is based on the principle of creating strong mental associations between new information and familiar, visualized locations. Doing so helps the brain to encode and retrieve information more efficiently.

Additionally, the technique is a form of active recall, which requires the user to actively engage with the information. This improves retention and recall. The method is also highly customizable. You can use it to memorize anything from numbers, names, historical facts, and even complex concepts. It's even been used by memory athletes to set world records in memorizing vast amounts of information. With the Memory Palace technique, you can take control of your memory and make it work for you[44].

Choose a place you can easily visualize for your first memory palace, such as the house where you grew up. As you need more rooms, create them based on familiar places.

Let's begin!

I have chosen to start with my front yard as my first "room" because it makes sense to me as a logical starting point. However, if a different room makes more sense to you, feel free to start there instead.

If you're having trouble coming up

with ideas, you can use my floor plan as inspiration, but you must be able to visualize the items in each room. It is crucial to imagine the room's furniture, windows, doors, and other details for this system to be effective.

After selecting a location for your room, begin by outlining the room. The drawing doesn't have to be perfect, just a representation of the room. In fact, my drawings often look like this:

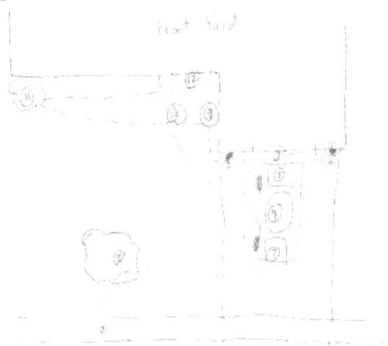

I'm not a great artist; however, I can still create something a little nicer for this book. Let's begin with the outline of my front lawn:

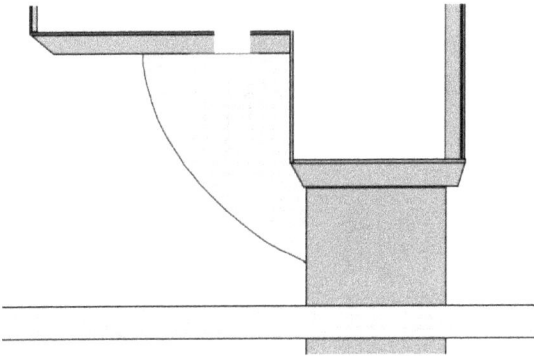

Next, I will place items that will serve as stopping points along our journey. I have added a couple of shrubs, a car, two house lights, a garage door, a front door, and two planters. Create as many stopping points as you need.

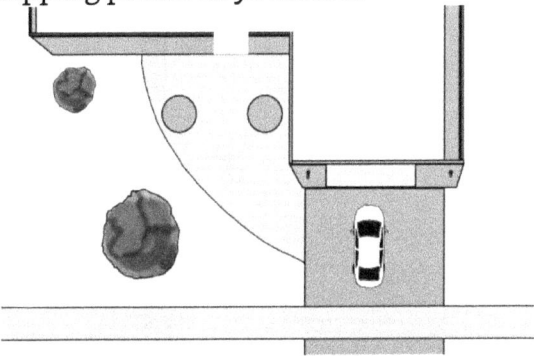

Third, number the spots from one to twelve. Create the path so that there is a logical organization. Make the route flow in one direction. It should be something you can easily remember and replicate.

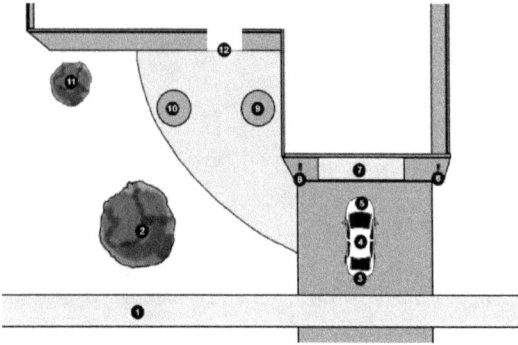

Finally, add the path that you will take from number to number. I like to imagine myself walking through the scene as I connect it all together. Here is my final image:

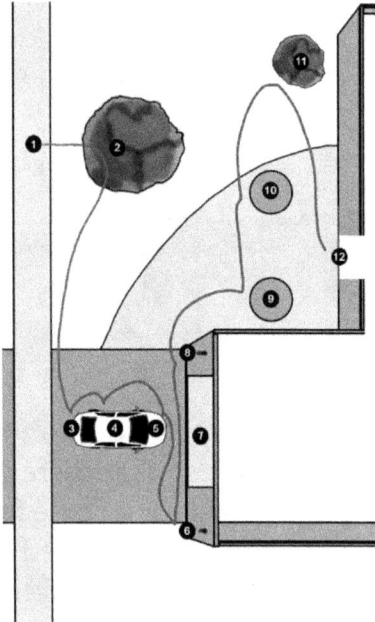

It is good to go through each room in your memory palace multiple times, making each location as vivid as possible in your mind. When we add information to each stop, our goal is to create dynamic, memorable scenes that come to life in our minds.

To do this, I create little stories for the things I want to store in each spot. I do this with the linking system and SAME principles.

Here is an example using this list of bones in the human hand:

1. Carpals
2. Scaphoid
3. Lunate
4. Triquetrum
5. Pisiform
6. Trapezium
7. Capitate
8. Hamate
9. Metacarpals
10. Phalanges

Spot One – Carpal

Stand in your first spot. Try to visualize it as clearly as possible. Imagine a giant blue carp standing around in your first spot. The blue carp jumps up and hugs you when you get close to it. It's your carp-pal! Make the image as big, colorful, and crazy as you can.

Spot Two – Scaphoid

In your second spot, imagine a ska band. They're dancing away in their weird checkered clothing until you get close to them. That's when they all collapse with typhoid fever. They're all lying on top of each other in a sweaty heap. They have "scaphoid."

Spot Three – Lunate

In your third spot, imagine a lunar eclipse. Take the eclipse and eat it! Chop it hard! You ate the lunar eclipse: lunate. You could also use a loon if you know what it looks like.

Spot Four – Triquetrum

For triquetrum, I have chosen to think about three people heavily smoking. Billows of smoke pour through their mouths. One of them says, I quit. The others agree. They throw their cigarettes on the ground and stomp them out. A moment later, one says, "Not today." The others agree and light up again. The three of them (tri) quit (quet) smoking. Triquet, and don't forget to take a sip of rum.

If this image doesn't work for you,

think of your own to put in spot four.

Spot Five – Pisiform

The next one is a little strange. When you get to your fifth spot, two people are having a pissing contest! Even though they are perverts, they have incredible form! They are pisiform.

Spot Six – Trapezium

In spot six, you ask yourself, "Has the circus come to town?" A trapeze artist is doing somersaults in the air. That should be enough to trigger the word trapezium.

Spot Seven – Capitate

The next spot is a little sad. There is someone stuck in a guillotine. Depending on how gruesome you want to make the image, you can end there, knowing that they will be decapitated, or imagine the scene playing out until it's bloody and gross. Just remember to remove the "de," and you have the word you're looking for: capitate.

Spot Eight – Hamate

In the eighth spot, imagine finding a big ol' leg of ham. Grab it. Eat it up. That's hamate.

Spot Nine – Metacarpal

In this spot, a giant orange carp rushes up to you. It shakes your hand and says, "Pleased to meet you!" You've just met-a-carp-pal!

Spot Ten – Phalanges

Fans of The Office will appreciate this one. Phyllis and Angela from The Office are hanging out in spot number ten. They're playing patty cake and waiting for you to join them!

And that's how we combine the linking system with a memory palace. It is the best way to remember anything for the long term. Simply walk through your memory palace occasionally to keep it fresh.

The Major System

The Major system is used to improve the memorization and recall of numbers, playing cards, and even dates. Some memory historians claim that the Major system was first developed by the German memory researcher Major Bartlomiej Beniowski in the early 19th century[45]. He is said to have spent years experimenting with different techniques, honing his skills, and perfecting the system. However, others argue that the true origins of the Major system lie with historian Johann Winkelmann (also known by the pseudonym Stanislaus Mink von Wennsshein) in 1648[46]. He is said to have stumbled upon the technique while trying to find a way to remember important dates in history.

The Major system is based on the idea that it is easier to remember meaningful words rather than random numbers. It involves using consonant sounds to represent numbers and adding vowels to form words. This way, instead of remembering a string of numbers, you can recall a term that is associated with those numbers. The system has been refined over the years, and Aime Paris published a version of the Major system in 1825 closer to its current form.

Whether its origins lie with Major Bartlomiej Beniowski or Johann Winkelmann is trivial. One thing is certain, though, the Major system is a powerful tool that can help anyone improve their memory and recall of all things numerical.

For example, the number 42 can be converted into the image of a "rune" (4 is given the sound "r" and 2 is given "n"). To memorize a phone number, you can associate each digit with a corresponding image and then link those images together meaningfully. You can use this technique to remember any numerical information, including credit card numbers, social security numbers, and dates in history.

This system converts numbers into consonant sounds and then adds vowels to form words. At first, this system might seem a little daunting. It will take some work to master the technique. Once you have worked it out, your ability to recall numbers will astound others.

An Example

The number that I want to remember is 53101740039633.

At the foot of my driveway, an angry **lama** stood in wait. Every few seconds, he gave the **tase**r in his hand a little test, listening to the sound of fifty-thousand volts shoot between the leads.

Finally, he saw his enemy lying in wait across the hood of my car: the **taco**. The lama rushed forward and zapped the taco. With the job done, the lama **race**d towards the front door, only to be met by the bartender from Cheers, **Sam** Malone.

Sam **push**ed the lama over. Proud of himself, Sam turned the handle and opened the door, where a **mime** stood guard.

Simplified, it goes: **L**a**ma tase**d a **taco**, then **race**d to the door. **Sam push**ed the lama over. He opened the door and met a **mime**.

That consonant sounds "l m t s t c r (soft c = s) s m p sh m m" is how I remembered the number: 53101740039633.

How it Works

In the example above, I've utilized three different systems to make the number vivid and memorable.

I used the link system and SAME principles to organize and make the scene enjoyable. Although it's out of context, I used a memory palace to add location. And I applied the Major system to remember the numbers themselves.

If you apply these three principles to any number, you'll be amazed at what you can remember. With only a little review, this sequence of numbers could stick with you for years! That might not be particularly useful for this random string of numbers. Still, it could be helpful to remember a social security number, credit card number, phone number, or anything with numbers!

When I go through the recall process, I'm not trying to remember numbers. I'm trying to recall a little story about the angry lama. It's so much easier than remembering random numbers. Recollecting stories is how memory masters can recite pi to tens of thousands of numbers. The current world record is 100,000 digits, set by Akira Haraguchi in 2006.

The chart below illustrates the typical letter-consonant relationship utilized in the Major system. These number-consonant pairs have been used for a long time. They have proven to be highly effective in helping individuals improve their memory and recall.

Each number is paired with a specific consonant sound. For example, the number "1" is typically associated with the letter "t" or "d" because they have a similar straight, vertical shape. Similarly, the number "2" is associated with the letter "n" because it has a similar curved shape.

The chart below contains the consonant-letter relationships that have been used for a long time. Please note that this is flexible. You can use any letter-consonant pair that works for you.

The key is to find the associations that make sense and that you can easily

Number	Consonant Sound	Rationale
0	s, z, soft c	Sounds similar to the z in zero.
1	t, d	Uses the same downstroke as in 1.
2	n	A tilted 2 looks similar to n.
3	m	A tilted 3 looks similar to m.
4	r	The last letter in four is r.
5	l	L is the Roman numeral for 50.
6	sh / ch	The reasons are terrible, so let's say "just because."
7	k, hard c	A capital K has two 7s in it.
8	f, v	A cursive F looks similar to 8.
9	p, b	P is the mirror image of 9.

remember.

Once we've converted numbers to letters, we can begin forming word associations. This can be done in two ways: by converting numbers to letters and creating word associations in real-time or using a pre-set list of images to encode the numbers beforehand. The latter method may be more effective because it can prevent stumbling and forgetting the mental pictures during the association process.

The vowels do not affect the associations, as they are considered "wildcards." It is important to choose words that are easy to visualize for the associations; for example, the number 1 could be associated with the word "toe" or "tea."

When creating permanent associations for numbers, it's common to use only the first ten digits (0-9). However, suppose a large set of numbers need to be memorized. In that case, it may be more effective to create associations for the numbers 00-99. Memory athletes who compete may need associations for even more numbers, up to 1000. However, creating associations for a thousand numbers is unnecessary for general use.

We'll use a simple number, 32, to demonstrate three different ways to complete the same task. Hopefully, it will help you decide which one is right for you.

Option One

First, we break down 32 into single digits and apply the corresponding consonants from the Major list above.

3 = m
2 = n

From here, we can create whatever word, or words, we like. As long as we use the corresponding consonant sounds.

Some options include men, main, moon, mono, and moan.

When we decode the letters, we look for consonant sounds and translate them back to numbers.

m = 3
n = 2

In this model, you choose whatever words you want, using a consistent number-consonant relationship, as stated in the above chart.

Option Two

We can perform this same task by using a list of words corresponding to the digits. We're still using the Major system, but we're also cutting out some of the work you would have to do as you memorize the numbers.

Here is the list of digits from 0 – 9 that you could draw from:

0 – Sauce
1 – Toe
2 – Neo (From the Matrix)
3 – Me
4 – Ray
5 – Lay
6 – Jaw
7 – Key

8 – Foe

9 – Pa

Now, we can break down 32 into:

3 = Me

2 = Neo

So, my image involves Me and Neo hanging out. I must create a vivid scene to make the numbers stick. Hopefully, you can see the benefit of having a list like this.

Option Three

While option three requires the most work initially, it will help you easily remember impressive lists of numbers once it's in place. We use the same process as in option two, except the list runs from 00 – 99. We have to memorize a hundred images to correspond with the digits. But it's worth it!

In the same example, the number 32 is represented by *moon*. Remembering 32 is as simple as making the moon explode in your mind. Here is the complete list of keywords from 00 to 99:

Double Digit List

00 – Sauce

01 – Stew

02 – Snow

03 – Sam
04 – Sari
05 – Sail
06 – Sushi
07 – Suck
08 – Sieve
09 – Sap
10 – Tase
11 – Teat
12 – Tuna
13 – Team
14 – Tree
15 – Tail
16 – Teach
17 – Taco
18 – Toffee
19 – Toilet Paper
20 – Nose
21 – Nut
22 – Nan
23 – 'Nam (Like Viet Nam)
24 – Nero
25 – Nail
26 – Nacho
27 – Neck
28 – Nave
29 – Nap
30 – Maze
31 – Mat
32 – Moon
33 – Mime

34 – Mare

35 – Mail

36 – Mash

37 – Make

38 – Move

39 – Mop

40 – Race

41 – Rat

42 – Rain

43 – Ram

44 – Rear

45 – Roll

46 – Rash

47 – Rock

48 – Rave

49 – Rap

50 – Lose

51 – Laid

52 – Lane

53 – Lama

54 – Lure

55 – Lily

56 – Leech

57 – Lick

58 – Laugh

59 – Leap

60 – Cheese

61 – Shit

62 – Chain

63 – Chum

64 – Chair

65 – Chill
66 – Cha-cha
67 – Check
68 – Chef
69 – Shape
70 – Kiss
71 – Cat
72 – Can
73 – Came
74 – Car
75 – Kill
76 – Cash
77 – Kick
78 – Cough
79 – Cab
80 – Face
81 – Fight
82 – Fan
83 – Foam
84 – Fair
85 – Fall
86 – Fish
87 – Fake
88 – Fife
89 – Fab
90 – Pass
91 – Pet
92 – Pan
93 – Puma
94 – Par
95 – Peel

96 – Push
97 – Pack
98 – Puff
99 – Peep

All three options have their pros and cons. Creating associations in real time allows for more flexibility and the ability to create more memorable stories. Still, it also increases the likelihood of making mistakes. A smaller, ten-number system is an excellent in-between strategy that works with medium-sized numbers to remember.

The benefit of using a more extensive hundred-number system is that it allows you to store twenty numbers with just ten images. However, it may take more time to memorize the chart. Ultimately, it's a personal choice, and you should decide which method works best.

When choosing images to associate with numbers, it's essential to make them as vivid and memorable as possible. You can use techniques like SAME (substitution, absurdity, movement, and exaggeration) to make the images stand out. Additionally, try to make the images as bright and striking as possible. Once you have your associations between numbers and words, you can create a story with them and then store them in a memory palace to help with recall later on.

Try to convert the following numbers into images (and back!) for practice:

Five Digits
64865
67173
35554
28929
55703

Six Digits
446339
551398
161612
500043
457004

Seven Digits
1055115
1505135
7225835
4023567
4817744

Eight Digits
10072082
59885115
78490499
57039383

95980413

Nine Digits
752858431
339642350
767189779
810012265
650999865

Ten Digits
7369870539
6992254508
8077877468
1819411904
5174558629

Twelve Digits and More!
632648595828
73172018768547
1418083445368522
958489993626299591
73944022453627202053
7032581144809186163684
923063955386114000670477909
149180181262259532156490646465
5

240608992181269664628138880640
2582330817683

332662356739222527004592174498
5824374011003519049961

Remember Important Dates

This memory technique for historical dates would have been helpful during my high school years. I had a passion for history, particularly when it came to wars and gladiators. However, I had difficulty remembering dates and specific information.

To start, we will focus on encoding the years. Once we have mastered that, we can incorporate months and days.

Step One

First, we'll use the Major system once again. Here is our association list:

0 – s, z, soft c
1 – t, d
2 – n
3 – m
4 – r
5 – l
6 – sh, ch
7 – k, hard c
8 – f, v
9 – p, b

Step Two

The following examples demonstrate how to use the Major system to convert the last three digits of a year into letters. We will not be including the first digit, as it is usually easy to remember in which millennium the event occurred. If you need to remember the millennium as well, you can use the Major system to include an additional consonant in the association.

We will work with three different events as examples:

1454 Creation of the Gutenberg Printing Press

1765 The American Revolution Begins

1346 The Black Death Begins

Transcribing the numbers we get:

Creation of the Gutenberg Printing Press

4 = r

5 = L

4 = r

The American Revolution Begins

7 = k/c

6 = sh/ch

5 = L

The Black Death Begins

3 = m

4 = r

6 = sh/ch

Step Three

The next step is to create memorable

words or phrases associated with the event we want to remember. This way, when we need to recall the date of an event, the image related to the event will trigger the memory of the date.

In this process, some people use multiple consonant sounds to represent numbers in a single word. However, I have found this to be inconsistent and potentially confusing. It increases the risk of making mistakes if one heavily relies on this method. Additionally, some consonant sounds may not align with the numbers you wish to remember.

To avoid these issues, I only use the first consonant sound of a word to represent the associated number. This method is consistent and straightforward. However, it's a personal preference. You may find that using a single word or a word with multiple consonants works better. Find a method that works best for you and practice it consistently.

Now, let's encode these numbers:

Creation of the Gutenberg Printing Press
4 = r = Rolling
5 = l = Lithographic
4 = r = Reprinter

Imagine a steamroller made of stone, like something out of the Flintstones. On the stone roller, a painting is etched out. As it rolls by, it makes reprint after reprint of the image wherever it goes. This is the rolling lithographic reprinter. The first letter of each word is tied to the Major system. Using the Major system, the consonant sounds I want are r, l, and r from the rolling lithographic reprinter. I need to add the millennium, and I have the date the Gutenberg press was made: 1454.

The American Revolution Begins
7 = k/c = Cavalry
6 = sh/ch = Charging
5 = l = Loons

Near the water's edge, an American cavalry division charges at a group of loons. If we remember the millennium, the rest is as easy as recalling cavalry charging loons. The c in cavalry represents 7, the ch in charging represents 6, and the l in loons represents 5. That gives us 1765.

The Black Death Begins
3 = m = Meerkats
4 = r = Retail

6 = sh/ch = Shamen

In a crowded market, meerkats are vendors. One particular meerkat sells shamen. The shamen are supposed to prevent the black death, but it kills people instead. The m in meerkats represents 3, the r in retail represents 4, and the *sh* in shamen represents 6. The black death started in 1346.

Now, to add months and days, we will combine elements from the Major system and a series of images to represent each month. While it might seem tedious to memorize a chart of months so that we can memorize dates, I promise you that the payoff is significant. Remembering historical dates will be much easier after you have this system in place.

We will put it all together using the UK release date of the Beatles' Magical Mystery Tour on November 19th, 1967.

Step One

First, we need to come up with our chart. Each image should be relevant and meaningful to you. The list below works for me. You can change any pictures if you know it will work better for you.

January = A snowy field
February = Cupid / a cherub

March = A soldier marching

April = A pill

May = Flowers

June = A Junebug (or any bug!)

July = Fireworks

August = A gust of wind blowing something over

September = A school

October = A witch

November = Turkey

December = A Christmas Tree

Again, this list works for me. If you can substitute better mental images, then you should. For now, we are concerned with November, represented by a turkey.

Step Two

For the day of the month, we will use the Major system. Here is our major system chart:

0 = s, z, soft c

1 = t, d

2 = n

3 = m

4 = r

5 = l

6 = sh, ch

7 = k, hard c

8 = f, v

9 = p, b

As we come across a day to remember, we encode the day into a word. For example, if the event happened on the 19th, our corresponding sounds are t and p. If we use the suggestion from the Major system chart, this will be fun! Imagine wrapping your image in toilet paper to remember a date!

Step Three

Create an image for the year using the Major system.

In this example, I will use 1967. I will break down 967 like this:

9 = p

6 = ch

7 – k

I am going to break this down into pee and chick.

Step Four

Combine all the images to form a date. Add a mental picture of the thing you want to remember. I want to remember the UK release date for the Beatles' Magical Mystery Tour. Here is what I have:

Begin with a turkey walking around. Wrap the turkey in toilet paper. There is a stream of pee splashing on the turkey's head. Following the pee, you find a chick(en) on a ladder. The chick is bathed in a rainbow that leads to the album cover for the Magical Mystery Tour.

My order is specific. If you prefer a different order, decide what works best for you — and stick with it! The order you choose isn't that important, but consistency is. I learned to use month, day, year, and event. I have stuck with that order ever since.

Decoding the Message
Working from our image to our date, we can decode our date.

Turkey = November

Toilet paper = 19

Pee(ing) chick = (1)967

The album cover of the Magical Mystery Tour doesn't require any further decoding.

On November 19, 1967, the Magical Mystery Tour album was released in the UK.

The process of remembering historical dates using this method may seem like extra work, but it is more effective than repeatedly reading the date and hoping it will eventually stick. After the date has been encoded, it becomes much easier to recall the associated images.

In conclusion, the linking method, memory palaces, and the Major system are powerful tools that can enhance our memory capabilities. By creating vivid and memorable associations between information and images, we can easily recall the information even after a long period. These techniques may take time and practice to master, but the effort is well worth it. With the ability to remember more, we can take on new challenges, achieve our goals, and make the most of every opportunity that comes our way. Remember, our most incredible power is the power of our minds, so let's use it to its fullest potential.

THE LAST TEST

Let's have one more test to check on our progress. If you utilize the tools discussed throughout the book, your abilities will certainly have improved. You may have noticed that we are also back at full-width text columns!

Good luck with your last test. I hope that you have found improvement in your reading speed and comprehension.

Just before you start reading, begin timing yourself. Stop your timer as soon as you are done. The reading score formula will be at the end of the reading selection. There will be ten comprehension questions and answers.

Let's begin!

Pets are beloved members of many families and households, providing companionship, love, and entertainment for their owners. While there are many different types of pets to choose from, some are more popular than others. In this article, we will take a look at the most preferred pets in the United States.

Dogs are arguably the most popular pet in the United States. They are known for their loyalty, intelligence, and ability to form strong bonds with their owners. Many different breeds of dogs are available, each with its own unique characteristics and personalities. Whether you are looking for a small lap dog or a large working dog, there is a breed to suit your needs.

Cats are another popular pet in the United States. They are known for their independent nature and are often preferred by people who are not home as much as they would like to be. Cats are also known for their grooming habits and their ability to catch small rodents and insects.

Fish are also a popular pet in the United States. They are known for their calming presence and their ability to improve the air quality in a room. Fish tanks are also a unique way to decorate a room and make it more interesting.

Birds are also a popular pet in the United States. They come in many different shapes, sizes, and colors. Many people like to keep birds as pets because they are very intelligent and can be taught tricks. Some people also enjoy the singing of birds, and many of them are great at it.

Reptiles and small animals like guinea pigs, hamsters, and rabbits are also popular pets in the United States. They are often preferred by people who have limited space or are looking for a low-maintenance pet.

One of the main reasons why people enjoy keeping pets is for the companionship and emotional support they provide. Pets, especially dogs and cats, have a way of understanding and comforting their owners in a way that no human can. They provide a sense of security and can help reduce feelings of loneliness and isolation.

Pets also have a therapeutic effect on their owners. Studies have shown that interacting with pets can lower blood pressure, decrease anxiety, and improve overall mental health. For example, petting a dog or cat can release oxytocin, a hormone associated with happiness and relaxation.

Pets can also be a source of entertainment and joy for their owners. Watching a fish swim in an aquarium or a bird singing can be mesmerizing and provide a sense of peace. For children, pets can also be a great learning opportunity, teaching them about responsibility, empathy, and compassion.

Additionally, owning a pet can be beneficial for one's physical health, as they provide the opportunity for their owners to engage in outdoor activities such as going for walks, running and playing with them.

In conclusion, there are many reasons why people enjoy keeping pets. From providing companionship and emotional support, to improving mental and physical health, pets bring many benefits to the lives of their owners. It's important to remember that owning a pet is a big responsibility and one should carefully consider their lifestyle and ability to provide for the animal before getting one.

Stop the timer!

To determine your current reading speed, do the following:

Divide 543 by the number of minutes it took you to read the selection.

543 words / ___ minutes = ____ wpm

That is your current reading speed.

Now, let's test your comprehension. Answer ten questions on the content of the article.

1. What are two of the most popular pets in the United States?
2. What are some characteristics of dogs that make them a popular pet choice?
3. Why are cats a popular pet choice?
4. What are some benefits of keeping fish as pets?
5. What are some advantages of keeping small animals like guinea pigs, hamsters, and rabbits as pets?
6. Why do people enjoy keeping pets?
7. How do pets provide emotional support for their owners?
8. What are some therapeutic benefits of interacting with pets?
9. What are the benefits of owning a pet for one's physical health?
10. What should be considered before getting a pet?

Answers:

1. Any of the following: dogs, cats, fish, birds, reptiles, and small animals like guinea pigs, hamsters, and rabbits are among the most popular pets in the United States.
2. Dogs are known for their loyalty, intelligence, and ability to form strong bonds with their owners.
3. Cats are known for their independent nature and are often preferred by people who are not home as much as they would like to be.
4. Fish are known for their calming presence and their ability to improve the air quality in a room.
5. Small animals are often preferred by people who have limited space or are looking for a low-maintenance pet.
6. People enjoy keeping pets for companionship and emotional support, for the therapeutic effects on their mental and physical health, for entertainment and joy.
7. They provide a sense of security and can help reduce feelings of loneliness and isolation.
8. Interacting with pets can lower blood pressure, decrease anxiety, and improve overall mental health.

9. Owning a pet can be beneficial for one's physical health as they provide the opportunity for their owners to engage in outdoor activities such as going for walks, running and playing with them.

10. Before getting a pet, one should carefully consider their lifestyle and ability to provide for the animal.

Mark your score out of   /10.

PRACTICE, PRACTICE, PRACTICE

In conclusion, *Read Faster Remember More* has provided you with valuable insights into the importance of using proper eye fixation, chunking, previewing, mnemonic techniques, and concentration during the reading process. These strategies, when implemented effectively, can significantly improve your reading speed and retention of information. Reading is a skill that can be developed and improved upon with practice. It is not a talent that one is born with but rather a skill that can be honed through consistent effort and dedication.

Proper chunking allows you to read more efficiently by reducing the number of times your eyes have to move over the page. Reducing sub-vocalization helps omit the middle man of the inner voice, which throttles our speed and ability to remember text. Previewing enables you to anticipate and prepare for the information you will encounter, making it easier to understand and retain. Mnemonic techniques provide a framework for organizing and remembering information, making it easier to recall later. And concentration is the key to keeping your focus on the task at hand and avoiding distractions.

Practice is essential to achieving success in any field or endeavor. Whether learning a new skill, perfecting a craft, or improving performance in sports or other activities, practice is the key to progress.

One of the main benefits of practice is that it helps to build muscle memory. When we repeat an action or movement repeatedly, our brains become more efficient at performing that action, and it becomes second nature. This is why athletes, musicians, and performers spend hours rehearsing and honing their skills each day. While our brains are organs, not muscles, the principle is the same. We strengthen our ability to learn when we practice learning.

Practice also helps to improve focus and concentration. When we are first learning something new, it can be challenging to stay focused and pay attention for long periods of time. However, as we practice more, our brains become better able to filter out distractions and stay focused on the task at hand.

Another critical aspect of practice is that it allows us to identify and overcome our weaknesses. As we repeat a task or movement, we may notice areas where we struggle or make mistakes. By focusing on these areas during practice, we can work to improve them and become stronger overall.

Finally, practice helps to build confidence. Our confidence grows as we become more proficient at a task or skill. This confidence can carry over into other areas of our lives, helping us tackle new challenges with ease and less anxiety.

Speed reading is no different from other skills. It requires practice to maintain and improve upon what you can accomplish. When it comes to speed reading, practice is crucial. The more you practice, the better you will become at reading quickly and efficiently.

By continually using these techniques and pushing yourself to read faster and remember more, you will be amazed at the progress you can make. With dedication and persistence, you will find that you can read and remember more than you ever thought possible. Remember, the more you read, the more you know, and the more you know, the more you can accomplish. So, take the time to practice these techniques, and you will soon find that you are reading faster and remembering more than ever before. Happy reading!

BIBLIOGRAPHY

1. Frank, Stanley D. The Evelyn Wood Seven-Day Speed Reading and Learning Program. Barnes & Noble, 1994.
2. Dellis, Nelson. Remember It!: The Names of People You Meet, All of Your Passwords, Where You Left Your Keys, and Everything Else You Tend to Forget. Skyhorse Publishing, Inc, 2016.
3. Yousafzai, Malala. "Malala's Story." Malala Fund, https://malala.org/malalas-story.
4. "Helen Keller." Encyclopædia Britannica, Encyclopædia Britannica, Inc., https://www.britannica.com/biography/Helen-Keller.
5. "Marie Curie." Encyclopædia Britannica, Encyclopædia Britannica, Inc., https://www.britannica.com/biography/Marie-Curie.
6. Sutz, Richard, and Peter Weverka. Speed Reading for Dummies. Hoboken: Wiley, 2009.
7. Peek, Fran, and Lisa Hanson. The Life and Message of the Real Rain Man: The Journey of a Mega-Savant. Dude Pub., 2008.
8. Buzan, Tony. The Speed Reading Book. London: BBC Active, 2007.
9. Marku, Anisa. The Art of Setting Smart Goals:

Set Winning Goals and Live a Life of Abundance, Success, and Achievement. Amazon Digital Services, 2019.

10. Jarrett, Christian. Great Myths of the Brain. Wiley Blackwell, 2015.

11. Medina, John. Brain Rules: 12 Principles for Surviving and Thriving at Work, Home and School. Pear Press, 2014.

12. Ibid.

13. Ibid.

14. Miller, G. A. (1956). The magical number seven, plus or minus two: Some limits on our capacity for processing information. Psychological Review, 63(2), 81–97. https://doi.org/10.1037/h0043158

15. Medina, John. Brain Rules: 12 Principles for Surviving and Thriving at Work, Home and School. Pear Press, 2014.

16. Jarrett, Christian. Great Myths of the Brain. Wiley Blackwell, 2015.

17. Medina, John. Brain Rules: 12 Principles for Surviving and Thriving at Work, Home and School. Pear Press, 2014.

18. Adler, Mortimer and Charles Van Doren. How to Read a Book. New York: Simon & Schuster, 1972.

19. Buzan, Tony. The Speed Reading Book. London: BBC Active, 2007.

20. Ostrov, Rick. The Power of Speed Reading. New York: Random House, 2016.

21. Marks Beale, Abby. The Ultimate Guide to Speed Reading. New York: Penguin, 2013.

22. Johnson, Toni. Speed Reading: Techniques,

Tips and Strategies. London: Kogan Page, 2015.

23. Frobose, Mark. Speed Reading Mastery. California: Language of Learning, 2002.

24. Buzan, Tony. The Speed Reading Book. London: BBC Active, 2007.

25. Ibid.

26. Frank, Stanley D. The Evelyn Wood Seven-Day Speed Reading and Learning Program. Barnes & Noble, 1994.

27. Rosenberg, Robert S. Sleep Soundly Every Night, Feel Fantastic Every Day: A Doctor's Guide to Solving Your Sleep Problems. DemosHealth, 2014.

28. Dandapani. Power of Unwavering Focus. Penguin Publishing Group, 2022.

29. Ibid.

30. Medina, John. Brain Rules: 12 Principles for Surviving and Thriving at Work, Home and School. Pear Press, 2014.

31. Robbins, Anthony. Awaken the Giant within: How to Take Immediate Control of Your Mental, Emotional, Physical & Financial Destiny! Simon & Schuster Paperbacks, 2013.

32. Hamilton, Jon. "Think You're Multitasking? Think Again." NPR, NPR, 2 Oct. 2008, https://www.npr.org/2008/10/02/95256794/think-youre-multitasking-think-again.

33. Wolpert, Stuart. "What Do We Lose When We Multitask?" University of California, 24 Aug. 2017, https://www.universityofcalifornia.edu/news/what-do-we-lose-when-we-multitask.

34. Faus, Ashley. "5 Diagrams That Show How Context Switching Saps Your Productivity." Work Life by Atlassian, Atlassian, 17 Mar. 2022, https://www.atlassian.com/blog/productivity/context-switching.

35. Jast, Joanna. Laser-Sharp Focus: A No-Fluff Guide to Improved Concentration, Maximised Productivity and Fast-Track to Success. Joanna Jast, 2016.

36. McKenna, Paul, and Michael Neill. I Can Make You Smarter. Bantam, 2012.

37. Brand, Willemien, et al. Visual Thinking: Empowering People & Organizations through Visual Collaboration. BIS Publishers, 2021.

38. Ibid.

39. Ibid.

40. Miller, G. A. (1956). The magical number seven, plus or minus two: Some limits on our capacity for processing information. Psychological Review, 63(2), 81–97.

41. Foer, Joshua. Moonwalking with Einstein: The Art and Science of Remembering Everything. Penguin Press, 2012.

42. Herrick, James A. The History and Theory of Rhetoric an Introduction. Routledge, 2021.

43. O'Brien, Dominic. How to Develop a Brilliant Memory Week by Week. Watkins Publishing, 2014.

44. Andrews, Conrad. Unlimited Learning: Amazing Memory for Adults. Cosmic Teapot Publishing, 2022.

45. Foer, Joshua. Moonwalking with Einstein: The Art and Science of Remembering Everything. Penguin Press, 2012.
46. Buzan, Tony. The Memory Book: How to Remember Anything You Want. BBC Active, 2010.

ABOUT THE AUTHOR

Conrad Andrews

About The Author Conrad Andrews Conrad Andrews struggled as a young student. It wasn't until grade twelve that he found memory techniques to help him with education. Since then, he has studied memory, focus, speed reading, and other Unlimited Learning techniques.

After getting a degree in computer science and his teaching qualifications, Conrad started teaching computer science in high school. Now, he shares both his love of computer science and Unlimited Learning strategies with his high school students.

Continue your learning journey with Conrad by signing up for the Unlimited Learning mailing list at: https://cosmicteapot.net/accelerated-learning/

Join the Unlimited Learning Facebook page at: https://www.facebook.com/ConradAndrewsUnlimitedLearning/

BOOKS BY THIS AUTHOR

Unlimited Learning: Amazing Memory For Adults

I understand what it's like to struggle with learning new information. Even my teachers thought I was "the slow kid" in school. It wasn't until grade twelve that I stumbled on memory techniques. After learning these simple skills, I went to college and earned a degree in computer science. Now, I teach high school students how to program computers using the same Unlimited Learning systems I would like to show you.

In this book, I've laid out easy step-by-step processes to help you unleash your learning abilities. Learn memory systems to store and retrieve:
Vocabulary words
Numbers
Dates
Speeches

Literature and more!

www.ingramcontent.com/pod-product-compliance
Lightning Source LLC
LaVergne TN
LVHW051046080426
835508LV00019B/1731